ideals

W9-DCA-999

Egg and Cheese
COOKBOOK

by Darlene Kronschnabel

Ideals Publishing Corp.
Milwaukee, Wisconsin

Contents

ISBN 0-8249-3009-6

Copyright © MCMLXXXII by Darlene Kronschnabel
All rights reserved.
Printed and bound in the United States of America

Published by Ideals Publishing Corporation
11315 Watertown Plank Road
Milwaukee, Wisconsin 53226
Published simultaneously in Canada

Associate Editor   Cover recipe:
and Food Stylist   Basic Omelet, page 43
Susan Noland

CREDITS

A very special thank you to the following for their cooperation and help in supplying selected recipes from their test kitchens and files:

American Blue Cheese Association, American Dairy Association of Wisconsin, American Egg Board, American Lamb Council, Beatrice Foods, Best Foods, California Apricot Advisory Board, California Plum Commodity Committee, California Raisin Advisory Board, California Table Grape Commission, Campbell Soup Company, Castle & Cooke Foods/Dole Bumble Bee, Del Monte Kitchens, Dudley-Anderson-Yutzy Public Relations, Durkee Foods, General Foods Consumer Center, General Mills, H. J. Heinz Foods, Idaho-Oregon Onion Promotion Committee, Idaho Potato Commission, Kelloggs, Meadow Gold Dairies, National Livestock and Meat Board, Norseland Foods, Inc., The Nestle Company, Inc., Oklahoma Peanut Commission, Pet, Inc., Rice Council of America, R. T. French, Stokely-Van Camp, Inc., Sunkist Growers, Inc., Sunsweet Prune Kitchen, Tuna Research Foundation, United Dairy Industry Association, Washington Asparagus Growers Association, Wisconsin Cheese Festivals, Wisconsin Department of Agriculture, Wheat Flour Institute.

Egg & Cheese Basics

EGGS: VERSATILE INFLATION FIGHTERS

When it comes to measuring up as a good food buy, eggs fit the requirements perfectly! Eggs contain high-quality protein and provide all vitamins, except C, along with thirteen important minerals, including iron, phosphorus and magnesium . . . for only 80 calories each!

Eggs are incredibly versatile, too. You can fry, poach, bake or scramble them, or cook them in their shells. Eggs can leaven soufflés or thicken sauces and custards. Eggs also bind ingredients, as in meat loaf, coat foods for frying, emulsify and clarify. It's no wonder that one famous French chef called eggs "the cement that holds the castle of cuisine."

The main reason egg prices are low is efficiency in breeding and raising hens, and collecting and processing the eggs. Today's egg suppliers house thousands of hens at just-right temperatures with carefully controlled lighting and feeding. In most modern egg operations, conveyor belts gather the eggs. Washing, weighing, grading and packing are all done by machine.

GRADING (FRESHNESS) AND SIZING

The primary difference between Grade AA and Grade A eggs is freshness, which translates into appearance when the egg is broken and taste when it is cooked. Under the best conditions, an egg could be Grade AA for seven to eight days after laying. It could be Grade A for an additional six weeks. The government grade is based on the cleanliness of the shell, soundness of the shell, thickness of albumin and size of the air cell. The grading of eggs has nothing to do with size; therefore, Grade AA eggs may be jumbo, extra large, large, medium or small.

The sizing of eggs is based on weight as follows:

JUMBO eggs weigh 30 ounces per dozen
EXTRA LARGE eggs weigh 27 ounces per dozen
LARGE eggs weigh 24 ounces per dozen
MEDIUM eggs weigh 21 ounces per dozen
SMALL eggs weigh 18 ounces per dozen

(All recipes in this book were tested using large eggs.)
Eggs kept under refrigeration at 45 to 55°F retain their inherent high quality for several weeks. Eggs kept at 72 to 80°F (room temperature) will lose more quality in one day than they will lose in one week under refrigeration.

Hard-cooked eggs can be refrigerated either in the shell or out. If the shell is removed, eggs should be protected in a film wrap. Dehydration and darkening of cooked egg white can be prevented by keeping eggs covered with water in a closed container. Use within 7 to 10 days.

HARD-COOKED EGGS

Cold Water Method: Cover eggs with water in pan to come at least 1 inch above eggs. Bring rapidly to boiling. Turn off heat and, if necessary, set pan off burner to prevent further boiling. Cover and let stand 15 minutes. Cool promptly and thoroughly in cold water; this makes the shells easier to remove and helps prevent a dark surface on yolks.

Boiling Water Method: Bring enough water to cover eggs in pan to rapid boiling. To avoid cracked shells, place cold eggs in warm water, prior to placing in boiling water. Transfer eggs to water with spoon, turn off heat, and, if necessary, set pan off burner to prevent further boiling. Cover and let stand 20 minutes. Cool as above.

Eggs peel more easily when the following procedures are observed:

1. Puncture shell at large end of egg before cooking.
2. Use either the hot water or cold water methods for hard-cooking (not boiling).
3. Do not overcook.
4. Cool immediately and thoroughly.
5. Crackle shell well before peeling.
6. Start peeling at large end of egg, placing under running water as may be necessary to ease off shell.

CHEESE: PERFECT ALONE OR WITH ANY MEAL

You don't have to be a cheese lover to know that this versatile dairy food has had a tremendous effect on all of us. For example, cheese has added wonderful words to our vocabulary with names like Gorgonzola and Gouda. Countries from Italy to Switzerland claim national cheese favorites. Cities such as Cheddar, Muenster, Parma, Rome and Limburg have cheeses named after them!

Shapes of cheese are nearly as numerous as the varieties; slices and slabs, wheels and wedges, bricks and blocks, cylinders and rounds are among popular choices.

Cheeses run the spectrum of colors from orange to creamy white to white; from yellow to blue to tan. Cheeses can be very hard, hard, semisoft or soft. Flavors range from mild to sharp.

Cheese contains protein, calcium, phosphorus and vitamin A. It is one of nature's most versatile foods, nutritious and readily digested.

Cheese can be served as a snack, in sauces, dips, desserts, seasonings, sandwiches, salads or casseroles. Cheese can fit your dining needs!

CHEESE STORAGE

Refrigerator: Cured cheeses keep well in the refrigerator for several weeks. Long holding will result in some additional curing and a sharper flavor.

Cheese should not be kept outside of the refrigerator for extended periods. Exposed to air and heat, cheese dries out, "oils-off" and might become moldy. Proper storage at 40°F preserves the original flavor and appearance and insures full use of the cheese without waste. Original wrapping, waxed paper, transparent wrap, aluminum foil and plastic bags are all satisfactory for refrigerator storage. Cover tightly to exclude air.

Natural cheeses when improperly wrapped or under moist conditions may develop mold spots. This harmless mold can be scraped off and no change in flavor will be noticed unless the mold had penetrated deeply into cracks in the cheese. In such cases the molding portion should be discarded. With blue cheese, however, the flavor comes from the molding process.

Cheese that has dried out may be grated and kept in a covered container in the refrigerator.

Freezer: Most natural cheese can be successfully frozen for 6 weeks to 2 months, if unopened, in the original package. Neufchatel does not freeze well. Partially used packages of natural cheese should be rewrapped and kept frozen only 6 weeks; pasteurized process cheeses can be frozen for 4 months. Freeze cheese in pieces of 1 pound or less, not over 1 inch thick, and wrap them tightly in moistureproof wrap to prevent loss of moisture and subsequent drying. After removing cheese from freezer, let thaw in refrigerator for 24 hours; use it soon after thawing.

CHEESE IDENTIFICATION AND DESCRIPTION

Name	Consistency and Basic Ingredient	Color, Shape, Flavor
BLUE	Semisoft; whole milk	White, marbled with blue-green mold; wheel; piquant, spicy
BRICK	Semisoft; whole milk	Light yellow to orange; brick-shaped; mild
CAMEMBERT	Soft; whole milk	Edible white crust, creamy yellow interior; small wheels; mild to pungent
CHEDDAR (AMERICAN)	Hard; whole milk	Nearly white to orange; varied shapes and styles, with rind and rindless; mild to sharp
COLBY	Hard type but softer than Cheddar; whole milk	Light yellow to orange; cylindrical; mild
COTTAGE	Soft; skim milk	White; packaged in cuplike container; mild, slightly acid
CREAM	Soft; cream and whole milk	White; foil wrapped in rectangular portions; mild, slightly acid
EDAM	Hard type but softer than Cheddar; partly skimmed milk	Creamy yellow with red wax coat; cannonball shape; mild, nutlike
FARMERS (PRESSED, POT)	Soft; whole or partly skimmed milk	White; dry cottage cheese pressed into parchment paper packages; mild
GORGONZOLA	Semisoft; whole milk	Light tan surface, light yellow interior, marbled with blue-green mold; cylindrical; piquant, spicy
GOUDA	Hard type but softer than Cheddar; partly skimmed milk	Creamy yellow with or without red wax coat; round and flat; mild, nutlike
LIMBURGER	Soft; whole or partly skimmed milk	Creamy white; rectangular; robust, highly aromatic
MONTEREY (JACK)	Semisoft; whole milk	Creamy white wheels; mild
MOZZARELLA	Semisoft; whole or partly skimmed milk	Creamy white; rectangular and spherical; mild, delicate
MUENSTER	Semisoft; whole milk	Yellow, tan or white surface, creamy white interior; small wheels and blocks; mild to mellow
NEUFCHATEL	Soft; whole milk	White; foil wrapped in rectangular portions; mild
PARMESAN	Hard; partly skimmed milk	Light yellow with brown or black coating; cylindrical; sharp, piquant
PROVOLONE	Hard; whole milk	Light golden yellow to golden brown, shiny surface bound with cord, yellowish-white interior; pear, sausage and salami shapes; mild to sharp and piquant
RICOTTA	Soft; whey and whole or skim milk, or whole or part skim milk	White; packaged fresh in paper, plastic or metal containers, or dry for grating; bland but semisweet
ROMANO	Hard; partly skimmed milk	Black coating; round with flat ends; sharp, piquant
SWISS (EMMENTALER)	Hard; partly skimmed milk	Rindless blocks and large wheels with rind; sweet, nutlike

This information was compiled with the help of the American Egg Board, the American Dairy Association and Wisconsin Cheese Festivals.

Appetizers & Beverages

Swiss Nibblers

Makes approximately 40.
Preparation Time: 40 minutes.

- 2 cups flour
- 1 tablespoon instant minced onion
- 1 teaspoon salt
- ½ teaspoon Italian seasoning
- ⅔ cup shortening
- 4 to 8 tablespoons cold water
- Swiss Beef Filling

Preheat oven to 425°. Stir dry ingredients together. Cut in shortening until pieces resemble coarse crumbs. Sprinkle with water, one tablespoon at a time, mixing lightly until dough begins to stick together. Press into a ball. Divide in half. Roll each half on a lightly floured surface into a circle ⅛ inch thick. Cut crackers with 2½-inch round cookie cutter. Place ¼ to ½ teaspoon Swiss Beef Filling in center of each circle. Brush edges lightly with water. Fold to half-circle, pressing edges to seal. Place on ungreased baking sheet. Bake 10 to 15 minutes or until lightly browned. Serve hot.

Swiss Beef Filling

- ¼ pound ground beef
- 1 teaspoon instant minced onion
- ⅛ teaspoon salt
- ⅓ cup shredded Swiss cheese
- ⅓ cup finely crumbled blue cheese
- 1 egg, beaten

Brown beef in skillet with onion and salt. Drain off excess fat. Stir in cheeses and egg.

Cheese Croquettes

Makes 4 servings.
Preparation Time: 35 minutes.

- Vegetable oil for deep frying
- 1 cup grated Monterey Jack cheese
- ½ cup dry bread crumbs
- 1 tablespoon butter
- 1 egg
- ½ teaspoon bottled steak sauce
- ¼ teaspoon ground sweet basil
- ¼ teaspoon ground thyme
- Paprika
- Salt and pepper to taste, optional

Heat oil to 375°. Combine remaining ingredients in bowl; mix well. Using a tablespoon, form mixture into croquettes. Fry until golden brown. Drain well.

Fried Cheese

Makes 2 dozen wedges.
Preparation Time: 20 minutes.

- ½ cup flour
- ½ cup milk
- 1 egg
- ½ teaspoon butter or margarine, melted
- ¼ teaspoon salt
- Pinch pepper
- 2 6-ounce packages Gruyere cheese
- ¾ cup fine, dry bread crumbs
- 3 to 4 tablespoons butter or margarine, for frying

Mix flour, milk, egg, ½ teaspoon butter, salt and pepper until smooth. Cut cheese into small wedges; dip in batter. Coat evenly with bread crumbs. Melt 2 tablespoons butter in a heavy skillet over low heat. Fry cheese wedges until golden brown. Add more butter to skillet as necessary. Drain on paper toweling. Spear with toothpicks; serve.

Cheesy Puffs

Makes 3 dozen.
Preparation Time: 45 minutes.

- ½ cup water
- ¼ cup butter
- ¼ teaspoon salt
- ¼ teaspoon dry mustard
- ½ cup flour
- 2 eggs
- ½ cup finely shredded Norvegia cheese
- 4 ounces Nokkolost cheese, cut in ¾-inch cubes
- 1 egg, lightly beaten
- 1 tablespoon sesame seed

Preheat oven to 450°. Combine water, butter, salt and mustard in small saucepan. Heat until mixture boils. Remove from heat. Add flour; blend until mixture forms solid mass. Add eggs, one at a time, beating well after each addition. Beat in shredded cheese. Drop mixture by rounded teaspoonfuls onto lightly greased cookie sheets. Bake 10 minutes. Reduce heat to 350° and bake 5 to 7 minutes. While still hot, cut a thin slice from the top of each puff. Place a cube of Nokkolost cheese in each cavity. Cover with top of puff. Brush each top with beaten egg; sprinkle with sesame seed. Return to oven; bake an additional 2 to 3 minutes. Remove from oven and serve immediately.

Cheesy Puffs
Swiss Nibblers
Sharp Edam Cheese Spread, page 8

Appetizers & Beverages

Ham Deviled Eggs

Makes 12 egg halves.
Preparation Time: 20 minutes.

 6 hard-cooked eggs
 1 2¼-ounce can deviled ham *or* ¼ cup
   finely chopped cooked ham
 3 tablespoons mayonnaise
 1 tablespoon prepared mustard
 ⅛ teaspoon onion powder
   Paprika

Cut eggs in half; remove yolks and mash well. Add ham, mayonnaise, mustard and onion powder. Mix thoroughly. Spoon mixture into whites. Sprinkle with paprika.

Stuffed Gouda Cheese

Makes 4 to 6 servings.
Preparation Time: 15 minutes.

 1 Gouda cheese, room temperature
 ¼ cup sherry
 ½ teaspoon prepared mustard
 ½ teaspoon Worcestershire sauce
 ⅛ teaspoon salt
 ⅛ teaspoon onion salt
 ⅛ teaspoon garlic salt
   Few grains cayenne pepper

Cut a circle about 3 inches wide from top of cheese, cutting diagonally down into cheese. Carefully scoop out cheese, leaving a shell about ¼ inch thick. Chop cheese coarsely; yield should equal 1 cup. Place all ingredients in bowl; blend. Fill shell, replace top and chill. Bring to room temperature before serving.

Sharp Cheese Spread

Makes 1½ cups.
Preparation Time: 20 minutes.

 1 8-ounce round aged Edam *or* Baby Gouda
   cheese, room temperature
 ½ cup finely chopped smoked beef
 ¼ cup dairy sour cream
 2 tablespoons pickle relish
 2 teaspoons prepared horseradish
   Apple wedges
   Crackers

Slice top of wax on cheese into 8 sections, leaving sides and bottom intact. Peel wax back to form petals. Carefully remove cheese from shell. Beat cheese until smooth. Add beef, sour cream, pickle relish and horseradish. Fill shell. Serve at room temperature with apple wedges and crackers.

Cheese and Wine

Cheese and wine together provide an elegant yet easy way to entertain. The many varieties of both cheeses and wines and their combinations make stimulating party refreshments.

You can pair cheese and wine in perfect harmony with some simple guidelines. Neither flavor should dominate the other. Rich, tangy cheeses team most happily with full-bodied red wines. More delicately flavored cheeses are generally preferred with light white wines.

Some general affinities of cheese with wine: mild Cheddar, Swiss, Colby, Muenster or Jack are delightful when served with the "nutty" flavor of Dry Sherry or the herb flavors of Dry Vermouth.

Delicate Colby, Edam, Gouda and Jack cheeses are nicely accentuated by light white table wines such as Sauterne, Rhine or Chablis.

Flavorful tangy cheeses like sharp Cheddar, aged Swiss, smoky Provolone, aged Brick and Port du Salut are best complemented with red table wines that have a full body—Burgundy, Claret, Chianti and Rosé.

Robust-flavored sharp Cheddar, Bel Paese, Port du Salut and blue cheeses are especially good with dessert wines. Port, Muscatel, Tokay and Cream Sherry are suggested.

Cheese should be served at room temperature for best flavor. Plan on about 6 ounces of cheese and ⅓ to ½ bottle of wine per person. Provide plenty of knives to avoid mixing the flavors of the various cheeses.

Brandied Cheese Ball

Makes 1.
Preparation Time: 15 minutes.

 1 15½-ounce can pink salmon
 1 8-ounce package cream cheese, softened
 ½ tablespoon brandy
 ½ teaspoon garlic salt
 6 drops hot pepper sauce
 ½ cup chopped pecans *or* sunflower kernels

Drain salmon. Remove skin and cartilage. Mash well. Beat cream cheese until light and fluffy. Beat in brandy, garlic salt and hot pepper sauce until blended. Blend in salmon. Refrigerate until firm enough to form into a ball. Roll in pecans. Refrigerate until ready to serve.

Snappy Cheese Wafers

Makes 4 to 5 dozen.
Preparation Time: 2 hours 45 minutes.

1¼ cups flour
1½ teaspoons baking powder
½ teaspoon salt
2 cups shredded Cheddar cheese
½ cup butter
1 teaspoon Dijon-style mustard
½ teaspoon liquid hot pepper sauce

Blend flour, baking powder and salt together. Combine cheese with remaining ingredients. Mix in flour mixture with hands until dough forms a ball. Form into a 12-inch roll; wrap in waxed paper. Chill 2 hours or overnight. Slice ¼ inch thick; place on ungreased baking sheet. Bake at 350° 10 to 12 minutes or until lightly browned. Remove immediately from baking sheet; cool on wire rack. Serve plain or with dip.

Pineapple Smoothie

Makes 4 servings.
Preparation Time: 5 minutes.

½ cup cottage cheese
1 8-ounce can crushed pineapple in unsweetened juice, chilled
2 eggs
2 cups cold milk
Dash salt

Beat cottage cheese, pineapple, juice and eggs in a blender. Add milk and salt. Blend just until foamy. Serve immediately.

Deluxe Eggnog

Makes 3 quarts.
Preparation Time: 15 minutes.

8 eggs
¾ cup granulated sugar
½ teaspoon salt
1 to 2 tablespoons rum *or* brandy
1 teaspoon vanilla
2 quarts milk
1 cup whipping cream
Nutmeg to taste
Miniature candy canes, optional

Beat eggs at high speed until thick and foamy. Gradually add sugar and salt. Add rum and vanilla. Add milk gradually at low speed. Cover and chill. Just before serving, whip cream and fold into eggnog. Pour eggnog into punch bowl. Garnish with nutmeg and candy canes.

Apple Eggnog

Makes 1 gallon.
Preparation Time: 10 minutes.

3 quarts apple juice, chilled
14 eggs
½ cup granulated sugar
1 tablespoon lemon juice
Lemon slices to garnish

Blend apple juice, eggs, sugar and lemon juice thoroughly. Serve in clear glasses garnished with lemon slice.

Orangegg Shrub

Makes 1 serving.
Preparation Time: 5 minutes.

1 egg
1 cup fresh orange juice
1 scoop lemon sherbet

Beat egg and orange juice until thoroughly mixed (too much beating causes excessive foaminess). Pour into chilled glass. Top with lemon sherbet. Serve promptly.

Note: ¼ cup frozen concentrate and ¾ cup water may be substituted for fresh orange juice.

Lemony Nog

Makes approximately 3 cups.
Preparation Time: 5 minutes.

1 scoop lemonade flavor drink mix
1 egg
½ cup water
1 cup milk
4 large ice cubes

Combine all ingredients in blender. Blend at high speed until smooth. Serve immediately.

Grape Frothy

Makes 4 servings.
Preparation Time: 10 minutes.

1 cup milk
1 6-ounce can frozen grape juice concentrate
4 egg whites
¼ cup water
¼ cup granulated sugar
8 or 9 ice cubes

Blend milk, grape juice concentrate, egg whites, water and sugar in a blender container on high speed. Add ice cubes, one at a time, blending until just chopped. Serve in tall glasses with straws.

Fondues

Classic Swiss Fondue

Makes 3⅔ cups.
Preparation Time: 25 minutes.

4 cups shredded Swiss cheese
¼ cup flour
1 clove garlic, halved
2 cups dry white wine
½ teaspoon salt
¼ cup Kirsch *or* dry sherry, optional
½ teaspoon Worcestershire sauce, optional
　French bread, cubed
　Vegetable dippers
　Ham, cubed
　Shrimp, cooked and peeled

Toss cheese and flour together. Rub inside of 3-quart saucepan with garlic; discard garlic. Add wine and heat until bubbly. Add cheese, ½ cup at a time, over medium heat, stirring until cheese is melted. Add salt, Kirsch and Worcestershire sauce, if desired. Transfer to fondue pot. Serve with French bread cubes, vegetable dippers, ham cubes, or cooked shrimp.

Tomato Swiss Fondue

Makes approximately 4 cups.
Preparation Time: 25 minutes.

1¾ cups tomato juice
1 clove garlic, peeled
4 cups shredded aged Swiss cheese
3 tablespoons cornstarch
¾ teaspoon salt
½ teaspoon Worcestershire sauce
½ teaspoon crushed basil leaves
¼ cup tomato juice
　French bread, cubed

Heat 1¾ cups tomato juice with garlic in top of double boiler over boiling water until very hot. Remove garlic. Add cheese, a small amount at a time, stirring constantly, until melted. (At this point, cheese may not be thoroughly combined with tomato juice.) Combine cornstarch, salt, Worcestershire sauce and basil with ¼ cup tomato juice; stir into cheese mixture. Stir until smooth. Serve in fondue pot or chafing dish over warmer. Serve with chunks of French bread. If the fondue becomes too thick, stir in a little more tomato juice.

Fondue Gruyere

Makes 2 to 4 servings.
Preparation Time: 15 minutes.

½ cup dry white wine
2 cups diced natural Gruyere cheese
½ cup Kirsch
1 loaf French bread *or* 6 bagels, cut
　into 1-inch cubes

Heat wine, but *do not boil.* Add cheese, a little at a time, stirring constantly, until cheese is completely melted and bubbling. Stir in Kirsch; blend thoroughly. Serve in fondue pot over medium heat so that fondue bubbles, but *does not boil.* Serve with bread cubes.

Beer Cheese Fondue

Makes 6 servings.
Preparation Time: 20 minutes.

1 small clove garlic, halved
¾ cup beer
2 cups shredded process Swiss cheese
1 cup shredded sharp natural Cheddar cheese
1 tablespoon flour
　Dash hot pepper sauce
　Bagels, cubed

Rub inside of heavy saucepan with cut surface of garlic; discard garlic. Add beer and heat slowly. Coat cheese with flour. Gradually add cheese to beer, stirring constantly, until mixture thickens. *Do not boil.* Stir in hot pepper sauce. Pour into fondue pot; place over low flame on fondue burner. Spear cubed bagels with fondue forks; dip into cheese, swirling to coat. If mixture becomes too thick, stir in a little warm beer.

Hot Shrimp Fondue

Makes 2 cups.
Preparation Time: 15 minutes.

1 8-ounce package cream cheese, softened
1 10½ ounce can cream of shrimp soup
½ cup dairy sour cream
1 teaspoon prepared horseradish
¼ teaspoon Worcestershire sauce
　Shrimp, cooked and peeled, optional

Heat cream cheese, cream of shrimp soup, sour cream, horseradish and Worcestershire sauce in saucepan, blending thoroughly. Transfer to fondue pot; place over low heat. Garnish with cooked, peeled shrimp, if desired.

Fondues

Cheese Fondue

Makes 4 servings.
Preparation Time: 15 minutes.

    1 clove garlic, halved
    1 pound Swiss cheese, shredded
    2 cups dry white wine
    1 teaspoon dry mustard
    ⅛ teaspoon salt
    ⅛ teaspoon pepper
    2 tablespoons cornstarch
    2 tablespoons water
    1 tablespoon lemon juice
    1 loaf French bread, cubed

Rub bottom and sides of a heavy 3 quart saucepan with garlic; discard garlic. Add cheese, wine, mustard, salt and pepper. Cook over medium heat, stirring constantly, until cheese melts and mixture is blended. Mix cornstarch and water until smooth. Stir into cheese mixture. Add lemon juice. Bring to boil over medium heat, stirring constantly; boil 1 minute. Pour into fondue pot over low heat. Serve with bread cubes.

Baked Cheese Fondue

Makes 6 servings.
Preparation Time: 1 hour 25 minutes.

    4 eggs, separated
    ¾ cup milk
    2 cups shredded Cheddar cheese
    3 cups cubed white bread
    ½ teaspoon salt
    ½ teaspoon dry mustard
    ⅛ teaspoon pepper
    ¼ teaspoon cream of tartar

Preheat oven to 325°. Beat egg yolks at high speed in small mixing bowl until thick and lemon-colored, about 5 minutes. Heat milk and cheese in large saucepan over low heat just until cheese melts. Remove from heat; stir in bread cubes, salt, mustard and pepper. Blend in egg yolks. Beat egg whites and cream of tartar at high speed in large mixing bowl until stiff but not dry. Fold bread mixture into egg whites. Pour into greased 1½-quart baking dish. Set dish in 13 x 9 x 2-inch baking pan on oven rack. Fill pan with hot water to depth of 1 inch. Bake 55 to 60 minutes until knife inserted near center comes out clean.

Cheesy-Beef Fondue

Makes 6 servings.
Preparation Time: 20 minutes.

    ½ pound ground beef
    1 15-ounce can tomato paste
    1 tablespoon cornstarch
    4 cups shredded mozzarella or Scamorze cheese
    1 8-ounce carton creamed cottage cheese
    ½ cup dry white wine
    1 teaspoon salt
  1½ teaspoons oregano
    ¼ teaspoon freshly ground pepper
    1 loaf French or Italian bread, cubed with crust intact

Brown ground beef in a small skillet. Stir in tomato paste and cornstarch; heat thoroughly. Transfer to fondue pot; place over low heat. Stir in cheeses, a little at a time, until melted. Blend in wine. Stir in seasonings. Serve with bread cubes.

Italian Fondue

Makes 4½ cups.
Preparation Time: 25 minutes.

    3 cups shredded Cheddar cheese
    1 cup shredded Provolone cheese
    3 tablespoons flour
    ½ pound ground chuck
    1 15-ounce can tomato sauce
    ½ cup dry white wine
  1½ tablespoons Italian salad dressing mix
      Italian bread, cubed
      Vegetable dippers

Toss cheeses and flour together. Brown meat in a 3-quart saucepan; drain fat. Add tomato sauce, wine and salad dressing mix. Heat until bubbly. Add cheese, ½ cup at a time, over medium heat, stirring until cheese is melted. Transfer to fondue pot. Serve with bread cubes and vegetable dippers.

Baked Ham-Spinach Fondue

Makes 6 servings.
Preparation Time: 1 hour 30 minutes.

    1 10-ounce package frozen chopped spinach, cooked and drained
    2 cups ground or finely chopped ham
  1½ cups soft bread crumbs or cubes
    1 cup shredded Cheddar cheese
    1 cup milk
    ⅛ teaspoon pepper
    ⅛ teaspoon nutmeg
    3 eggs, separated

Preheat oven to 325°. Combine spinach, ham, bread crumbs, cheese, milk, pepper and nutmeg. Beat egg yolks well; stir into ham mixture. Beat egg whites until stiff; fold gently into mixture. Pour into a 1½-quart ungreased casserole. Bake 50 to 60 minutes or until firm.

Seafood Fondue

Makes 6 to 8 servings.
Preparation Time: 45 minutes.

    1 8-ounce package cream cheese, cubed
    ½ cup milk
    1 clove garlic, crushed
    ⅔ cup grated Parmesan cheese
    1 6½-ounce can minced clams, drained
    1 4¼-ounce can broken shrimp, drained
    1 6½-ounce can crab meat, drained and flaked
    2 tablespoons dry white wine
    ½ teaspoon Worcestershire sauce
      Fresh bread, cubed
      Vegetable dippers

Melt cream cheese in milk in saucepan over low heat, stirring until smooth. Blend in garlic, Parmesan cheese, clams, shrimp, crab meat, wine and Worcestershire sauce; cook 5 minutes. Pour into chafing dish; serve with bread and vegetable dippers. Add a little more wine if fondue thickens.

Pizza Fondue

Makes 16 to 20 servings.
Preparation Time: 20 minutes.

    1 onion, chopped
    ½ pound ground beef
    2 10½-ounce cans tomato sauce
    1 tablespoon cornstarch
    1½ teaspoons fennel seed
    1½ teaspoons oregano
    ¼ teaspoon garlic powder
    10 ounces Cheddar cheese, grated
    1 cup grated mozzarella cheese
      Garlic bread or French bread, cubed

Brown onion and ground beef in a large skillet. Mix tomato sauce and cornstarch together; add to ground beef mixture. Blend in fennel seed, oregano and garlic powder. Add Cheddar and mozzarella cheeses. Stir over medium heat until cheeses are melted. Pour into fondue pot. Serve with bread cubes.

Cheese 'N Apple Fondue

Makes 4 cups.
Preparation Time: 20 minutes.

    4 cups shredded Cheddar cheese
    1½ cups shredded Provolone cheese
    ¼ cup flour
    2¼ cups apple juice or cider
    ½ teaspoon nutmeg
      Apple, pear and melon chunks

Mix cheeses with flour. Heat apple juice in saucepan to boiling. Gradually stir in cheese. Stir constantly until cheese melts and forms a smooth mixture. Add nutmeg. Transfer to fondue pot. Keep warm over low heat. Serve with apple, pear and melon chunks.

Dessert Cheese Fondue with Fruit

Makes 6 servings.
Preparation Time: 25 minutes.

    1 pound seedless grapes, chilled
    1 large apple, chilled
    1 small pineapple, chilled
    1 8-ounce package cream cheese
    8 ounces Port Salut or other mild cheese, grated
    ½ cup dry white wine
      Dash nutmeg
      Pound cake, cubed

Wash and slice fruit. Melt cheese in wine in fondue pot over low heat, stirring until smooth and bubbly. Add nutmeg. Serve with sliced fruit and cake.

Strawberry Fondue

Makes 6 servings.
Preparation Time: 15 minutes.

    1 12-ounce package frozen strawberries, thawed
    1 3-ounce package cream cheese, softened and cubed
    2 teaspoons cornstarch
    2 tablespoons orange liqueur
      Cake, cubed
      Fruit, sliced

Place first 4 ingredients into blender; cover and blend until smooth. Pour into medium saucepan; cook over medium heat, stirring constantly, until smooth and thickened. Serve in fondue pot over low heat. Dippers may include cubes of angel food or sponge cake and doughnuts and assorted fruit slices.

Variation: Use frozen or canned peaches, raspberries or apricots in place of strawberries.

Sauces & Soups

Hollandaise Sauce

Makes approximately 1 cup.
Preparation Time: 15 minutes.

¾ cup butter
1½ tablespoons lemon juice
3 egg yolks
Dash salt
Dash cayenne pepper

Approximately 10 minutes before serving, place ¼ cup butter, lemon juice and egg yolks in top of double boiler. Cook slowly over hot, *not boiling,* water, beating constantly. Temperature of water must be *below* simmering. When butter is melted, add another ¼ cup butter; continue beating until sauce thickens. Add remaining ¼ cup butter; beat until butter is melted and sauce is thickened. Stir in seasonings. Serve immediately.

Note: If sauce begins to curdle, add hot water, 1 teaspoon at a time, beating vigorously until smooth.

Mornay Sauce

Makes approximately 2½ cups.
Preparation Time: 20 minutes.

¼ cup butter *or* margarine
3 tablespoons flour
1 teaspoon salt
⅛ teaspoon white pepper
2 cups milk
¼ cup grated Parmesan cheese
2 egg yolks, beaten

Melt butter in a small saucepan. Stir in flour, salt and pepper. Add milk gradually; cook over low heat, stirring constantly until thickened and smooth. Stir in cheese. Add a little of the hot mixture into yolks; add to remaining sauce, stirring constantly.

Eggnog Sauce

Makes 2 cups.
Preparation Time: 10 minutes

2 egg yolks, lightly beaten
¼ cup granulated sugar
1 teaspoon vanilla
Dash salt
1 cup heavy cream, whipped

Combine egg yolks, sugar, vanilla and salt; blend well. Fold mixture into whipped cream. Serve over fruit, puddings or pound cake.

Lemon Medley Sauce

Makes 3 cups.
Preparation Time: 20 minutes.

2 teaspoons grated lemon peel
½ cup fresh lemon juice
1½ cups granulated sugar
¾ cup butter
4 eggs, lightly beaten

Combine lemon peel, juice, sugar and butter. Cook over low heat until butter is melted and sugar is dissolved. Blend a small amount of hot mixture into eggs; return all to saucepan. Cook over medium heat, stirring constantly, until mixture thickens slightly. *Do not boil.* Cool. Serve on cake, pudding, ice cream or in tarts.

Fruit Sauce

Makes 4 servings.
Preparation Time: 15 minutes.

1 17-ounce can fruit cocktail
⅓ cup orange juice
1 tablespoon honey
2 teaspoons reconstituted lemon juice
2 teaspoons cornstarch
½ banana, sliced

Drain fruit cocktail, reserving 2 tablespoons liquid. Blend reserved liquid in saucepan with orange juice, honey, lemon juice and cornstarch. Cook over medium heat, stirring constantly, until thickened. Stir in fruit cocktail and banana; heat until warmed through.

Cheese Sauce

Makes 2⅔ cups.
Preparation Time: 15 minutes.

2 tablespoons butter
¼ cup flour
½ teaspoon salt
2 cups milk
½ teaspoon prepared mustard
1½ cups cubed sharp Cheddar cheese

Melt butter in a saucepan. Blend in flour and salt. Add milk slowly, stirring until smooth. Cook and stir until thickened. Add mustard and cheese. Stir over low heat until cheese melts. Keep warm. *Do not boil.*

Note: Use Cheese Sauce over cooked vegetables or with cooked potatoes, rice or noodles.

Cheese Sauce with Cauliflower

Sauces & Soups

Cheesy Shrimp Spaghetti Sauce

Makes 5 to 6 servings.
Preparation Time: 20 minutes.

- 1 4-ounce can sliced mushrooms, drained, reserve liquid
  Water
- 1 1½-ounce package spaghetti sauce mix
- 1 8-ounce can tomato sauce
- 2 tablespoons butter
- 1 6-ounce package frozen cooked shrimp, thawed, rinsed, and drained
- 1 cup shredded Provolone cheese
  Hot, buttered spaghetti

Add enough water to reserved mushroom liquid to make 1 cup. Combine spaghetti sauce mix and tomato sauce. Stir in liquid; add butter. Cook according to package directions. Add mushrooms and shrimp; stir in cheese just until melted. Serve over hot, buttered spaghetti.

Cottage Cheese Dessert Sauce

Makes 1 cup.
Preparation Time: 10 minutes.

- 1 cup large curd cottage cheese
- 1 tablespoon cream
- 1 tablespoon granulated sugar
- ½ teaspoon vanilla
- ½ teaspoon grated lemon rind
  Nutmeg, optional

Place all ingredients except nutmeg into blender. Blend until smooth and creamy. Add a dash of nutmeg if desired. Excellent topping for strawberries, peaches or pound cake.

Quick Vegetable-Egg Soup

Makes 4 servings.
Preparation Time: 30 minutes.

- 1 cup thinly sliced onion
- 1 cup peeled and thinly sliced carrots
- ⅛ teaspoon garlic powder
- 2 tablespoons butter
- 4 cups beef broth *or* 3 10½-ounce cans condensed beef bouillon soup, undiluted
- 4 ½-inch slices Italian *or* French bread, toasted and cubed
- 8 eggs
- ½ cup shredded Cheddar *or* Monterey Jack cheese

Sauté onion and carrots with garlic powder in butter 2 to 3 minutes. Add beef broth; bring to a boil. Reduce heat, cover and simmer 10 minutes. While broth is simmering, place bread cubes in 4 soup bowls. Break eggs, one at a time, into small dish; then ease each egg into simmering broth, tipping dish into the water's surface. Simmer 3 to 5 minutes, depending on desired firmness. Pour approximately 1½ cups soup into each bowl. Place 2 poached eggs in each bowl. Sprinkle with cheese.

Swiss Onion Soup

Makes 8 servings.
Preparation Time: 1 hour 20 minutes.

- ¼ cup butter
- 7 cups sliced onion
- 2 tablespoons flour
- ½ teaspoon salt
- 4 cups beef bouillon
- 2 cups milk
- 8 thick slices French bread, toasted and buttered
- 2 cups shredded Swiss cheese

Preheat oven to 350°. Melt butter in 4-quart saucepan. Sauté onion until tender. Stir in flour and salt; cook 1 minute, stirring constantly. Gradually stir in bouillon. Bring to a boil; reduce heat. Cover and simmer 30 to 40 minutes. Stir in milk. Heat thoroughly. *Do not boil.* To serve, ladle soup into ovenproof mugs or bowls. Top each with 1 slice French bread and ¼ cup Swiss cheese. Bake 10 minutes or until cheese melts.

Hearty Bean Soup

Makes approximately 3 quarts.
Preparation Time: 2 hours 45 minutes.

- 1 pound dried red kidney beans
- 2 quarts water
- 2½ cups chopped onion
- 6 carrots, cut into ½-inch slices
- 2 cups water
- 1 12-ounce can tomato paste
- 1 tablespoon chili powder
- 1 tablespoon salt
- 1½ teaspoons garlic salt
- ¼ teaspoon pepper
- 12 ounces Provolone cheese, cubed

Rinse beans. Cover with 2 quarts water in a large kettle. Bring to a boil. Boil 2 minutes. Cover; let stand 1 hour. Uncover and bring to boil. Cover and simmer 45 to 50 minutes or until beans are tender. Stir in vegetables, 2 cups water, tomato paste and seasonings; cover and simmer 30 to 35 minutes, or until carrots are tender. Stir cheese into hot soup just before serving.

Onion-Cheddar Soup

Makes 4 to 6 servings.
Preparation Time: 45 minutes.

   5 cups sliced sweet Spanish onion
⅓ cup finely chopped celery
⅓ cup finely chopped carrot
¼ cup butter *or* margarine
   2 tablespoons flour
   6 cups well-seasoned beef broth
½ teaspoon salt
   Dash pepper
1½ cups grated sharp Cheddar cheese
   Toast wedges

Sauté onion, celery and carrot in butter over low heat until translucent. Blend in flour. Gradually add broth, stirring until mixture boils. Cover; simmer over low heat 10 minutes. Add salt, pepper and cheese, stirring until cheese is melted. Serve with toast wedges.

Alpine Cheese Soup

Makes 7½ cups.
Preparation Time: 30 minutes.

   2 10¾-ounce cans cream of shrimp soup
½ teaspoon dry mustard
1½ soup cans milk
   1 8-ounce bottle beer
   1 teaspoon Worcestershire sauce
   1 10-ounce package frozen, cut asparagus
   2 cups shredded Swiss cheese

Blend soup and mustard in saucepan; add milk, beer, Worcestershire sauce and asparagus. Bring to boil; cover. Reduce heat; simmer 15 minutes. Add cheese; heat until cheese melts, stirring occasionally.

Cheesy Vegetable Soup

Makes 8 servings.
Preparation Time: 30 minutes.

¼ cup butter
½ cup minced onion
½ cup flour
¼ teaspoon baking soda
1¼ teaspoons salt
¼ teaspoon paprika
2½ cups milk
2½ cups chicken bouillon *or* broth
½ cup diced carrots
½ cup diced celery
¼ pound sharp Cheddar cheese, cubed
   1 tablespoon chopped parsley

Melt butter in a large saucepan; sauté onion. Add flour, baking soda and seasonings; blend

well. Slowly add milk and bouillon, stirring constantly until smooth. Add vegetables and cheese cubes. Simmer for 15 minutes or until vegetables are tender and cheese is melted. *Do not boil* or soup will curdle. Garnish with parsley.

Egg Chowder

Makes approximately 6 servings.
Preparation Time: 35 minutes.

   2 cups cubed, raw potatoes
   1 10¾-ounce can chicken broth
⅓ cup butter *or* margarine
¼ cup flour
   2 cups 2% milk
   1 16-ounce can whole kernel corn, with liquid
   1 16-ounce can green beans, with liquid
¼ cup chopped pimiento
   1 small onion, sliced in rings
¼ teaspoon pepper
   1 bay leaf
¾ cup diced Cheddar cheese
   9 eggs, hard-cooked and sliced
   Salt to taste

Simmer potatoes in chicken broth, covered, until just tender, about 10 minutes. Melt butter in a 3-quart saucepan over low heat. Stir in flour; cook until bubbly. Add milk; cook, stirring constantly, until smooth and thickened. Add potatoes, corn and beans, including liquid, pimiento, onion, pepper and bay leaf. Simmer 15 minutes to blend flavors; remove bay leaf. Add cheese, eggs and salt just before serving.

Egg Nuggets

Makes 10 small balls.
Preparation Time: 20 minutes.

   2 hard-cooked egg yolks
¼ teaspoon salt
⅛ teaspoon pepper
   1 egg white
   1 tablespoon flour
   2 tablespoons butter

Force egg yolks through a sieve; add salt, pepper and enough egg white to moisten. Shape into small balls; roll in flour. Sauté in butter until lightly browned. Drain on absorbent paper. Add to soup just before serving.

Salads

Frozen Fruit Cheese Salad

Makes 12 servings.

Preparation Time: 25 minutes; chill overnight.

    2 cups small curd cottage cheese
    1 cup dairy sour cream
    3 tablespoons confectioners' sugar
    ¾ teaspoon salt
    1 cup drained pineapple tidbits
    1 cup diced orange
    1 cup cooked, pitted, chopped prunes
    1 large banana, sliced
    ½ cup sliced maraschino cherries
    ½ cup chopped blanched almonds
       Salad greens
       Creamy Pink Dressing
       Maraschino cherries for garnish
       Orange sections for garnish

Blend cottage cheese in blender until smooth. Pour into a large mixing bowl. Mix cottage cheese lightly with sour cream, sugar, salt, pineapple, orange, prunes, banana, cherries and almonds. Pour into a 9 x 5 x 3-inch loaf pan, which has been rinsed in cold water. Freeze overnight until firm. Allow to stand a few minutes before cutting into serving pieces. Place on salad greens. Serve with Creamy Pink Dressing and garnish with a cherry and orange section.

Creamy Pink Dressing

Makes 1 cup.

Preparation Time: 5 minutes.

    1 cup dairy sour cream
    2 tablespoons maraschino cherry juice

Blend sour cream and juice; refrigerate.

Sweet 'n Sour Asparagus Salad

Makes 6 servings.

Preparation Time: 40 minutes.

    1 pound fresh asparagus spears, trimmed
    6 slices bacon
    ¼ cup wine vinegar
    2 teaspoons granulated sugar
       Dash salt
       Dash pepper
    2 green onions, finely chopped
       Shredded lettuce
    2 hard-cooked eggs, sliced

Cook asparagus in boiling salted water 8 to 10 minutes or until tender; drain. Cook bacon in skillet until crisp. Remove bacon, drain and crumble; set aside. Add vinegar, sugar, salt, pepper and onion to bacon drippings in skillet. Add asparagus; heat thoroughly. Place lettuce in 6 salad bowls. Arrange asparagus on lettuce. Top with egg slices. Pour vinegar dressing over salad. Sprinkle with bacon.

Medley Supper Salad

Makes 8 servings.

Preparation Time: 1 hour 10 minutes.

    2 cups cottage cheese
    1 cup dairy sour cream
    ½ teaspoon salt
    1 cup unpeeled sliced cucumber
    2 cups torn lettuce
    3 green onions, including tops, chopped
    ½ cup sliced radishes
    ½ cup sliced green pepper
    ½ cup thin diagonal slices celery
    2 hard-cooked eggs, quartered
       Cherry tomatoes, halved

Mix cottage cheese, sour cream and salt. Chill 1 hour. Cut cucumber slices in half; salt and chill. Drain before adding to salad. Line large salad bowl with lettuce and fill with cottage cheese mixture. Arrange cucumbers, onions, radishes, green pepper, celery, eggs and tomatoes on top. Toss together and serve.

Wilted Lettuce Toss

Makes 4 servings.

Preparation Time: 30 minutes.

    4 slices bacon
    4 cups torn leaf lettuce
    1 large tomato, chopped
    ¼ cup sliced green onion
    2 tablespoons vinegar
    ¼ teaspoon salt
       Dash pepper
    3 hard-cooked eggs, sliced

Fry bacon in skillet until crisp; drain, reserving 1 tablespoon drippings. Crumble bacon; set aside. Combine lettuce, tomato and onion. Heat reserved drippings, vinegar, salt and pepper in skillet to boiling. Gradually add lettuce mixture, tossing only until leaves are coated and wilted slightly. Place in serving bowl; top with crumbled bacon. Garnish with hard-cooked eggs. Serve immediately.

Marinated Vegetables, page 20

Salads

Egg Salad-Stuffed Tomatoes

Makes 4 servings.
Preparation Time: 20 minutes.

- 4 large tomatoes
- 4 hard-cooked eggs
  Mayonnaise
- 1 3-ounce can deviled ham
  Salt and pepper
  Lettuce
  Parsley

Cut slice from stem end of each unpeeled tomato. Scoop out pulp; turn tomatoes upside down to drain. Chop eggs; add tomato pulp and moisten with mayonnaise. Add ham, and salt and pepper to taste. Fill tomato shells with mixture. Serve on lettuce. Garnish with parsley.

Mushroom Salad

Makes 6 to 8 servings.
Preparation Time: 15 minutes.

- 2 cups sliced fresh mushrooms
- ½ cup Italian dressing
- 1 large tomato, coarsely chopped
- 1 cup julienne-sliced green pepper
- 1½ quarts torn crisp salad greens
- 2 ounces Greek feta cheese, crumbled

Toss sliced mushrooms with Italian dressing in a large salad bowl. Toss tomato with green pepper; add to mushrooms. Let stand 5 minutes. Add salad greens to vegetables, mixing well. Sprinkle feta cheese on top to serve.

Fruit-Cheese Salad

Makes 6 servings.
Preparation Time: 15 minutes.

- 4 medium apples, unpeeled and diced
- 1 medium banana, sliced
- ½ teaspoon salt
- 3 tablespoons lemon juice
- 2 tablespoons orange juice
- 1 cup drained pineapple tidbits
- 1½ cups green seedless grapes
- ½ cup coarsely chopped pecans
- 1 cup cottage cheese
- ¼ cup sour cream
  Salad greens

Sprinkle apples and banana with salt, lemon juice and orange juice. Add pineapple, grapes and pecans. Blend together cottage cheese and sour cream. Add to fruit mixture; toss lightly. Spoon onto crisp salad greens.

Greek Salad

Makes 8 servings.
Preparation Time: 15 minutes.

Dressing

- 1 8-ounce carton plain yogurt
- 1 tablespoon chopped parsley
- 1½ teaspoons garlic salad dressing mix
- 1 teaspoon lemon juice

Combine all ingredients, cover and chill to blend flavors. Pour dressing over salad just before serving.

Salad

- 2 quarts torn lettuce
- 1½ cups cubed Fontina cheese
- ¾ cup ripe olives
- 2 tomatoes, cut into wedges

Toss together all ingredients.

Marinated Vegetables

Makes 6 to 8 servings.
Preparation Time: 20 minutes; chill 2 hours.

- 2 cups cubed Jarlsberg cheese
- 1 cup sliced carrots
- 1 cup cauliflowerets
- 1 cup sliced celery
- 1 cup sliced mushrooms
- 1 cup cubed green pepper
- 1 cup halved cherry tomatoes
- 1 cup sliced zucchini
- ⅓ cup sliced green onions
- 3 tablespoons chopped parsley
- ⅓ cup Italian dressing
- ½ teaspoon dry mustard
  Salad greens, optional

Combine all ingredients, except salad greens, in large bowl. Toss well. Chill several hours; toss occasionally.

Creamy Egg Coleslaw

Makes 5 servings.
Preparation Time: 20 minutes.

- 4 hard-cooked eggs
- 4 cups finely shredded red cabbage
- 2 tablespoons finely chopped onion
- 2 tablespoons sweet pickle relish
- ½ cup mayonnaise
- 2 teaspoons prepared yellow mustard
- ½ teaspoon salt
  Dash pepper
  Paprika

Reserve two of the egg yolks; set aside. Chop remaining hard-cooked eggs into medium-sized pieces. Combine egg, cabbage, onion and pickle relish. Mix together mayonnaise, mustard, salt, and pepper. Toss coleslaw mixture with dressing. Place in serving bowl. Sieve the remaining hard-cooked egg yolks; sprinkle on salad. Sprinkle with paprika.

Pineapple Waldorf

Makes 6 servings.
Preparation Time: 20 minutes.

    1 20-ounce can pineapple chunks, drained, reserving 1 tablespoon syrup
    ½ cup coarsely chopped pecans
    ½ cup diced celery
    2 large apples, cored and cut in chunks
    ¾ cup crumbled blue cheese
    ⅓ cup mayonnaise
    3 cups salad greens
    2 tablespoons lemon juice

Combine pineapple, pecans, celery, apples, and ½ cup blue cheese. Toss together lightly. Blend syrup and mayonnaise. Add to salad mixture, tossing lightly. Arrange salad with greens on plates. Drizzle lemon juice on top. Garnish with remaining ¼ cup crumbled blue cheese.

Jellied Egg Salad

Makes 10 to 12 servings.
Preparation Time: 30 minutes to mix; chill overnight.

    2 3-ounce packages orange flavor gelatin
 1¼ cups boiling water
    2 cups cold water
    3 tablespoons lemon juice
    1 cup mayonnaise
    ¼ cup drained pickle relish
    ¾ teaspoon salt
    ¼ cup minced onion
    2 tablespoons finely chopped pimiento
    6 hard-cooked eggs, chopped, reserve 1 yolk
       for garnish

Dissolve gelatin in boiling water. Add cold water and chill in the refrigerator until slightly thickened. Stir in lemon juice, mayonnaise, pickle relish, salt, onion and pimiento. Fold in eggs. Spoon into 2-quart serving bowl. Chill overnight or until firm. Garnish with sieved egg yolk.

Cheese Dressing

Makes ¾ cup.
Preparation Time: 10 minutes.

    ¼ cup milk
    ½ cup mayonnaise
    ¼ cup grated Parmesan or crumbled blue cheese
       or finely shredded Cheddar cheese
    ¼ teaspoon Worcestershire sauce

Blend milk with mayonnaise. Mix in cheese and Worcestershire sauce. Chill. Serve with mixed green, citrus, egg or fish salads.

Cheese French Dressing

Makes 1½ cups.
Preparation Time: 15 minutes.

    ½ cup salad oil
    ¼ cup white vinegar
    ⅛ cup granulated sugar
    ¼ cup catsup
    ½ teaspoon salt
    ¼ teaspoon white pepper
    ½ teaspoon dry mustard
    2 tablespoons grated onion
    1 cup grated Cheddar cheese

Combine all ingredients and mix well.

Herb Dressing

Makes 1 cup.
Preparation Time: 10 minutes.

    ¾ cup mayonnaise
    1 hard-cooked egg, finely chopped
    2 tablespoons finely chopped parsley
 1½ teaspoons tarragon vinegar
    ½ teaspoon prepared mustard
    1 teaspoon finely chopped chives

Blend all ingredients. Chill. Serve with mixed greens, vegetables or meat salads.

Creamy Celery Seed Dressing

Makes 1 cup.
Preparation Time: 5 minutes.

    1 cup dairy sour cream
    ¼ cup milk
    2 hard-cooked eggs, sieved
    2 teaspoons chopped chives
 1½ teaspoons celery seed
    ½ teaspoon salt
    ½ teaspoon pepper
    2 tablespoons vinegar

Combine sour cream, milk, eggs, chives, celery seed, salt and pepper in a small bowl; mix well. Blend in vinegar.

Vegetables

Cauliflower with Cheese Sauce

Makes 4 servings.
Preparation Time: 35 minutes.

- 1 medium cauliflower, trimmed and washed
- ½ cup julienne-sliced ham
- 3 tablespoons butter *or* margarine
- 3 tablespoons flour
- 2 cups milk
- 1 teaspoon dry mustard
- ¼ teaspoon paprika
- ½ teaspoon salt
- ⅛ teaspoon pepper
- 1½ cups shredded Jarlsberg *or* Fjordland cheese
- 2 tablespoons chopped parsley

Boil cauliflower rapidly in lightly salted water until just tender. Brown ham in butter in saucepan. Add flour and cook 5 minutes over low heat, stirring, until smooth. Remove from heat; gradually blend in milk. Add seasonings and cheese. Cook, stirring constantly until sauce is thickened and smooth. Spoon over cauliflower in ovenproof dish. Broil until lightly browned. Garnish with parsley.

Scalloped Potatoes Florentine

Makes 6 servings.
Preparation Time: 1 hour 45 minutes.

- 1 10¾-ounce can condensed Cheddar cheese soup
- 1 16-ounce can tomatoes, drained and chopped
- 1 10-ounce package frozen chopped spinach, cooked and drained
- ½ cup sliced onion
- ½ teaspoon lemon juice
- ½ teaspoon crushed marjoram leaves
- ⅛ teaspoon garlic powder
- ⅛ teaspoon pepper
- 2 cups shredded Swiss cheese
- 4 cups thinly sliced potatoes

Preheat oven to 375°. Combine all ingredients, except ½ cup cheese and potatoes in a bowl. Alternate layers of potatoes and sauce in a buttered 2-quart casserole. Cover; bake for 1 hour and 10 minutes. Uncover; sprinkle with remaining cheese. Bake an additional 15 minutes.

Cheesy Broiled Tomatoes

Makes 4 servings.
Preparation Time: 20 minutes.

- 1 cup shredded Cheddar cheese
- 2 tablespoons flour
- 1 cup milk
- 1 teaspoon Worcestershire sauce
- ½ teaspoon dry mustard
- ¼ teaspoon garlic salt
- 10 drops yellow food coloring
- 4 large tomatoes, halved and broiled
  Chopped parsley

Toss cheese and flour together; set aside. Heat milk, Worcestershire sauce, mustard, garlic salt and food coloring in a saucepan over low heat. Add cheese, stirring constantly, until melted. Pour sauce over tomato halves. Garnish with parsley.

Nutty Peas

Makes 5 servings.
Preparation Time: 15 minutes.

- ¼ cup butter *or* margarine, melted
- 3 tablespoons flour
- 1 17-ounce can peas, drained, reserve liquid
  Water
- 2 tablespoons milk
- ½ teaspoon salt
- 1 cup pasteurized process cheese spread
- ¼ cup sliced blanched almonds

Combine butter and flour in saucepan. Add water to reserved liquid to equal 1 cup; stir liquid and milk into saucepan. Cook over medium heat, stirring constantly, until thickened and bubbly. Add salt and cheese; stir until cheese melts. Fold peas and almonds into sauce. Heat thoroughly.

Corn Pudding

Makes 6 servings.
Preparation Time: 1 hour.

- 2 8¾-ounce cans whole kernel corn, drained
- 2 eggs, lightly beaten
- ¾ cup evaporated milk
- 2 tablespoons butter *or* margarine, melted
- 1 teaspoon salt
- ⅛ teaspoon pepper

Preheat oven to 350°. Combine all ingredients in a medium bowl. Pour into a greased 1½-quart baking dish. Bake 45 minutes or until firm.

Vegetables

Cheesy Lemon Vegetables

Makes 6 servings.
Preparation Time: 25 minutes.

- **3 tablespoons butter** *or* **margarine**
- **2 tablespoons flour**
- **¼ teaspoon dry mustard**
- **⅛ teaspoon salt**
- **⅛ teaspoon paprika**
- **1 cup milk**
- **1 cup shredded Cheddar cheese**
  Juice of **½ lemon**
- **2 10-ounce packages frozen peas** *or* **chopped spinach, cooked, well drained**

Melt butter in saucepan; stir in flour, mustard, salt and paprika. Gradually add milk, stirring until mixture begins to thicken. Add cheese; stir until melted. Stir in lemon juice and peas; heat thoroughly.

Eggs in Tomato Jackets

Makes 6 servings.
Preparation Time: 25 minutes.

- **6 medium tomatoes**
- **2 tablespoons butter**
  Salt and pepper
- **6 eggs**

Preheat oven to 350°. Cut tops from tomatoes. Make a hollow in the center of each tomato large enough to hold 1 egg. Add 1 teaspoon butter, season with salt and pepper and break an egg into each. Bake until eggs are firm, about 20 minutes.

Cabbage Delight

Makes 6 servings.
Preparation Time: 1 hour.

- **1 medium head cabbage**
- **1 green pepper, julienne sliced**
- **1 cup boiling chicken broth**
- **¼ cup flour**
- **1 teaspoon salt**
  Dash black pepper
- **1 8-ounce carton cottage cheese, sieved**
- **½ cup sour cream**
- **2 tablespoons tomato paste**
- **½ cup chopped dill pickles**

Preheat oven to 350°. Rinse cabbage. Cut into 1-inch wedges; remove core. Simmer cabbage and green pepper in chicken broth for 7 minutes or until just tender. Arrange vegetables in a buttered 8-inch baking dish. Stir flour into broth. Add seasonings. Cook until thickened, stirring constantly. Blend in cottage cheese, sour cream and tomato paste. Add dill pickles. Pour sauce over vegetables. Bake for 30 minutes.

Broccoli-Stuffed Onions

Makes 6 servings.
Preparation Time: 50 minutes.

- **3 large sweet Spanish onions**
- **1 10-ounce package frozen chopped broccoli, cooked and drained**
- **¼ cup Parmesan cheese**
- **⅓ cup mayonnaise**
- **2 teaspoons lemon juice**
- **2 tablespoons butter** *or* **margarine**
- **2 tablespoons flour**
- **¼ teaspoon salt**
- **⅔ cup milk**
- **1 3-ounce package cream cheese, cubed**

Preheat oven to 375°. Peel and halve onions. Parboil in salted water 10 to 12 minutes; drain. Remove centers leaving ¾-inch edges. Chop center portions to equal 1 cup. Combine chopped onion, broccoli, Parmesan cheese, mayonnaise and lemon juice. Spoon into centers of onion halves. Melt butter in saucepan. Blend in flour and salt. Add milk; cook until thickened, stirring constantly. Remove from heat and blend in cream cheese until smooth. Spoon sauce over onion halves; bake, uncovered, 20 minutes.

Scalloped Asparagus

Makes 6 servings.
Preparation Time: 30 minutes.

- **2 cups fresh asparagus, cut into ½-inch diagonal pieces, cooked but still crisp,** *or* **1 10-ounce package frozen asparagus cuts and tips, thawed**
- **4 hard-cooked eggs, sliced**
- **3 tablespoons butter** *or* **margarine**
- **2 tablespoons flour**
- **¼ teaspoon salt**
- **⅛ teaspoon pepper**
- **1½ cups milk**
- **¼ cup bread** *or* **cracker crumbs**
  Paprika, optional

Preheat oven to 350°. Arrange asparagus and egg slices alternately in a 1-quart casserole dish. Melt 2 tablespoons butter in small saucepan. Stir in flour, salt and pepper. Slowly stir in milk. Heat to boiling. Boil 1 minute. Pour over asparagus. Combine crumbs and 1 tablespoon butter. Sprinkle over asparagus. Sprinkle with paprika. Bake 20 minutes or until crumbs are browned and casserole is bubbly.

Cranberry-Cheese Baked Yams

Makes 4 servings.
Preparation Time: 1 hour 45 minutes.

    4 medium-sized yams
    3 tablespoons butter or margarine
    1 cup canned whole cranberry sauce
    1 cup diced Cheddar cheese
    ¾ teaspoon salt
      Dash freshly ground pepper

Preheat oven to 350°. Bake yams 45 to 55 minutes or until tender. Scoop pulp from shells and mash with butter; beat until light and fluffy. Fold in cranberry sauce, cheese, salt and pepper. Spoon yam mixture lightly into shells. Bake 30 minutes.

Cheesed Potato Crisps

Makes 6 servings.
Preparation Time: 40 minutes.

    ¼ cup butter or margarine
    5 medium baking potatoes, pared, cut
      lengthwise into ¼-inch slices
      Salt
    1½ cups shredded pasteurized process
      American cheese
    2 cups crushed cornflakes
      Paprika

Preheat oven to 350°. Melt butter in 15½ x 10½ x 1-inch baking pan. Arrange potatoes in single layer in pan, turning once to coat both sides with butter. Sprinkle with salt, then with cheese. Top with crushed cornflakes; sprinkle with paprika. Bake 25 minutes or until fork tender.

Swiss Beans

Makes 6 servings.
Preparation Time: 40 minutes.

    2 tablespoons butter or margarine
    1 tablespoon flour
    ¼ teaspoon salt
      Dash pepper
    ½ teaspoon dry minced onion
    ½ cup dairy sour cream
    1 16-ounce can sliced French-style green beans,
      drained
    1 cup shredded Swiss cheese
    1 cup crushed cornflakes

Preheat oven to 350°. Melt 1 tablespoon butter in saucepan; add flour, salt, pepper, onion and sour cream. Gently stir in green beans; place in a 1-quart casserole. Sprinkle with cheese. Mix 1 tablespoon melted butter and cornflakes. Sprinkle over cheese. Bake, uncovered, 20 minutes.

Scrambled Eggs with Asparagus

Makes 6 servings.
Preparation Time: 10 minutes.

    6 eggs
    ½ cup asparagus tips, cooked
      Salt and pepper to taste
    1 tablespoon butter
      Hot buttered toast

Add eggs to asparagus; blend well. Season with salt and pepper. Melt butter in 10-inch skillet. Add egg mixture. Cook slowly over medium heat until eggs are set. Serve on hot buttered toast.

Rutabaga-Potato Casserole

Makes 6 servings.
Preparation Time: 1 hour 30 minutes.

    2 medium rutabagas, peeled
    2 medium potatoes, peeled
    ½ cup flour
    1 teaspoon baking powder
    1 teaspoon salt
    ⅛ teaspoon pepper
    4 eggs, beaten
    ¼ cup milk
    ¼ cup butter, melted

Preheat oven to 325°. Cover vegetables with cold water; let stand. Sift flour, baking powder and seasonings together. Blend ½ of dry ingredients with eggs; stir in milk and butter. Drain vegetables; grate in blender. Mix remaining dry ingredients with vegetables; add to egg mixture and blend well. Place mixture in greased 1-quart casserole. Set in pan; fill with hot water to ⅔ of the height of the casserole. Bake 1 hour.

Zucchini and Tomato Casserole

Makes 6 servings.
Preparation Time: 1 hour 30 minutes.

    2 cups sliced zucchini
    1 cup thinly sliced onion
    2 small tomatoes, sliced
    ⅓ cup fine bread crumbs
      Salt
      Pepper
    1 tomato, cut in wedges
    ½ cup grated Cheddar cheese

Preheat oven to 375°. In a 1½-quart casserole, layer half each of the zucchini, onion, tomatoes and bread crumbs; sprinkle with salt and pepper. Repeat layers. Top with tomato wedges. Cover; bake 1 hour. Uncover; sprinkle with cheese. Return to oven until cheese melts.

Golden Stuffed Pork Chops

Makes 6 servings.
Preparation Time: 1 hour 25 minutes.

   6 rib pork chops, 1 to 1½ inches thick
   1 small onion, finely chopped
   2 tablespoons butter *or* margarine
   ¾ cup cooked rice
   1 cup shredded Cheddar cheese
   1 teaspoon Worcestershire sauce
1¼ teaspoons salt
   ⅛ teaspoon pepper
   2 tablespoons lard *or* drippings

Preheat oven to 350°. Using a small sharp knife, make a pocket in each pork chop by cutting into the center of the chop from the rib side, parallel to the rib bone and the surface of the chop. For the stuffing, cook onion in butter until transparent and combine with rice, cheese, Worcestershire sauce, ¼ teaspoon salt and pepper. Fill each pocket with approximately 3 tablespoons stuffing. Lightly brown chops in lard. Sprinkle with 1 teaspoon salt, place on rack in roasting pan and cover securely with foil. Bake 30 minutes. Uncover and bake 30 minutes longer.

Cheesy Chicken

Makes 5 servings.
Preparation Time: 1 hour 35 minutes.

   1 2½ to 3½ pound frying chicken, cut into
      serving pieces, washed and patted dry
   ½ cup margarine
   1 cup flour
   ¾ cup grated Romano *or* Parmesan cheese
   ½ teaspoon salt
   ½ teaspoon pepper
   ½ teaspoon basil *or* garlic powder
   ¾ teaspoon paprika
   1 tablespoon onion flakes, optional
   2 eggs
6½ ounces evaporated milk

Preheat oven to 350°. Grease a cookie sheet with 1 teaspoon of the margarine. Melt remaining margarine in small pan and set aside. Mix flour, cheese, salt, pepper, basil, paprika and onion flakes together. Beat eggs and milk with fork until blended. Dip each chicken piece in egg-milk mixture; roll in flour and cheese mixture. Arrange on baking sheet, sprinkle remaining coating over chicken and pour melted margarine over top. Bake 60 to 75 minutes.

Mozzarella Meat Loaf

Makes 8 servings.
Preparation Time: 1 hour 15 minutes.

1½ pounds lean ground beef
   ½ cup dry bread crumbs
   1 egg, lightly beaten
   1 teaspoon instant minced onion
   ¾ teaspoon salt
   ½ teaspoon crushed oregano
   1 10¾-ounce can tomato soup
1½ cups shredded mozzarella cheese
   1 4-ounce can mushroom stems and pieces,
      drained, optional

Preheat oven to 375°. Grease 12 x 8 x 2-inch baking pan. Combine beef, bread crumbs, egg, onion, salt and oregano in mixing bowl. Stir in ¾ cup tomato soup. Cut a piece of waxed paper 15 inches long. Press meat into a 13 x 9-inch rectangle on waxed paper. Sprinkle meat with cheese; top with mushrooms. Starting with narrow end of meat, lift waxed paper to help roll meat jelly-roll fashion. Place meat, seam-side down, in prepared pan. Bake 30 minutes. Remove excess drippings from baking pan. Pour remaining soup over meat loaf. Bake an additional 30 minutes.

Chicken Kiev

Makes approximately 6 servings.
Preparation Time: 1 hour 30 minutes.

   ¾ cup butter
   ½ cup crumbled blue cheese
   1 clove garlic, pressed
   2 tablespoons chopped parsley
   2 tablespoons chopped chives
12 chicken breasts, skinned, boned
1½ cups flour
   1 teaspoon salt
   3 eggs, lightly beaten
      Vegetable oil, for deep frying
      Rice *or* noodles

Mix butter, cheese, garlic, parsley and chives together. Form into 12 small balls. Freeze about ½ hour. Pound chicken breasts to ¼-inch thickness. Roll chicken around butter-cheese balls. Secure edges with picks or skewers. Mix flour and salt together. Dip chicken pieces in flour, then in beaten egg, then again in flour. Deep fry chicken at 375° for 20 minutes or until golden brown. Do not pierce chicken. Serve with rice.

Main Dishes

Chicken Cordon Rouge

Makes 4 servings.
Preparation Time: 1 hour 10 minutes.

- 1 8-ounce can whole oysters
- 4 chicken breasts, split, skinned and boned
- 1 clove garlic, minced
- ½ cup diced onion
- 1 tablespoon butter
- 1 cup shredded Gruyere cheese
- 1 tablespoon chopped parsley
- 1 egg, beaten
- ¾ cup bread crumbs
- 2 tablespoons vegetable oil
- ½ cup water
- 1 teaspoon chicken stock base
- ¼ teaspoon salt
- ½ cup dairy sour cream
- 1 tablespoon flour
  - Hot fluffy rice
  - Parsley

Drain oysters, reserving liquid. Pound chicken breasts flat with a meat mallet to about ¼ inch thick. Sauté garlic and onion in butter until onion is soft. Combine oysters, sautéed vegetables, cheese and parsley. Spoon equal amounts of oyster mixture in center of each chicken breast. Fold sides to overlap filling; secure with toothpicks. Dip in egg and roll in bread crumbs. Brown chicken in oil in skillet, adding additional oil if necessary. Remove chicken; drain excess fat from skillet. Add reserved oyster liquid, water, chicken stock base and salt. Combine sour cream and flour. Stir into skillet until blended. Return chicken to skillet. Cover; simmer 30 minutes. Serve with hot fluffy rice. Garnish with additional parsley.

Bright Macaroni and Cheese

Makes 6 to 8 servings.
Preparation Time: 45 minutes.

- 2 cups elbow macaroni, cooked and drained
- 2 tablespoons butter *or* margarine
- ¼ cup chopped onion
- ½ cup chopped green pepper
- 2 tablespoons flour
- 2 cups milk
- 1 teaspoon salt
- ¾ teaspoon dry mustard
- ¾ teaspoon liquid hot pepper sauce
- 2 cups shredded sharp Cheddar cheese
- 1 tomato, peeled, seeded and chopped

Preheat oven to 350°. Melt butter in medium saucepan. Add onion and green pepper; sauté until tender. Blend in flour. Gradually stir in milk.

Add salt, dry mustard and liquid hot pepper sauce. Cook over medium heat, stirring constantly, until mixture thickens and comes to a boil. Add cheese and stir until melted. Remove from heat. Stir in tomato and macaroni. Pour into greased 1½- to 2-quart baking dish. Bake 20 to 25 minutes.

Cheese-Broiled Flank Steak

Makes 8 servings.
Preparation Time: 15 minutes.

- 1 2-pound flank steak
  - Salt and pepper
- 1 cup crumbled blue cheese

Sprinkle flank steak with salt and pepper. Broil 3 to 4 inches from heat, 5 to 6 minutes. Turn; broil 5 minutes. Sprinkle with cheese. Broil 2 minutes or until cheese is melted.

Beef Parmigiana

Makes 6 servings.
Preparation Time: 1 hour 30 minutes.

- 1½ pounds top round steak, ½ inch thick
- ⅓ cup dry bread crumbs
- ⅓ cup grated Parmesan cheese
- 2 eggs, beaten
- ⅓ cup vegetable oil
- 1 large onion, chopped
- 4 medium tomatoes, peeled and quartered
- 1 8-ounce can tomato sauce
  - Salt and pepper to taste
- 1 teaspoon crushed basil
- ½ teaspoon crushed oregano
- 1½ cups grated mozzarella cheese

Trim excess fat from steak; cut into 6 pieces; pound each piece with heavy mallet to about ¼-inch thickness. Combine bread crumbs and Parmesan cheese. Dip each piece of meat in beaten egg, then in crumb mixture. Heat oil in large skillet and brown steak well on both sides. Remove steak to paper towels; drain. Add onion, tomatoes, tomato sauce, salt, pepper, basil and oregano to skillet; stir to combine. Bring mixture to a boil; lower heat and simmer, uncovered, 30 minutes. Preheat oven to 350°. Spoon 5 tablespoons cooked tomato mixture into bottom of 13 x 9 x 2-inch baking dish. Place steak on top of sauce in single layer. Pour remaining sauce over steak; bake 1 hour. Remove from oven; sprinkle with cheese. Bake an additional 15 minutes or until cheese is melted.

Hot Turkey Salad Casserole

Makes 12 servings.
Preparation Time: 30 minutes.

4 cups cubed cooked turkey
2 cups chopped celery
2 cups seedless green grapes
2 cups mayonnaise
1 cup slivered almonds
1 4-ounce can sliced mushrooms, drained
¼ cup lemon juice
1 teaspoon salt
1 teaspoon soy sauce
1 cup shredded colby cheese
2 cups crushed potato chips
  Cranberry relish
  Rolls

Preheat oven to 450°. Mix first 9 ingredients together; pour into 13 x 9 x 2-inch baking dish. Cover with cheese; top with potato chips. Bake 15 minutes to melt the cheese and blend flavors. Serve hot with cranberry relish and rolls.

Lasagne

Makes 12 servings.
Preparation Time: 2 hours 20 minutes.

2 pounds ground beef
¾ cup chopped onion
1 clove garlic, minced
1 16-ounce can tomatoes
1 15-ounce can tomato sauce
2 tablespoons parsley flakes
2 tablespoons granulated sugar
1 teaspoon salt
1 teaspoon crushed basil
3 cups creamed cottage cheese
½ cup grated Parmesan cheese
1 tablespoon parsley flakes
1½ teaspoons salt
1 teaspoon crushed oregano
1 8-ounce package lasagne noodles, cooked and drained
¾ pound mozzarella cheese, shredded
½ cup grated Parmesan cheese

Preheat oven to 350°. Cook beef, onion and garlic in large saucepan or Dutch oven until meat is browned and onion is tender. Drain off all fat. Add tomatoes; break up with fork. Stir in tomato sauce, 2 tablespoons parsley flakes, sugar, 1 teaspoon salt and basil. Heat until mixture boils, stirring occasionally. Reduce heat; simmer, uncovered, 1 hour. Mix cottage cheese, ½ cup Parmesan cheese, 1 tablespoon parsley flakes, 1½ teaspoons salt and oregano. Reserve ½ cup meat sauce for top layer. In ungreased 13 x 9 x 2-inch baking pan layer one-quarter each of the noo-dles, meat sauce, mozzarella cheese and cottage cheese mixture; repeat three times. Spread reserved meat sauce over top; sprinkle with ½ cup Parmesan cheese. If desired, lasagne can be covered and refrigerated several hours at this point. Bake uncovered 45 minutes.

Ham-Rice Casserole

Makes 8 to 10 servings.
Preparation Time: 1 hour.

6 tablespoons butter
1½ cups regular, long grain rice, uncooked
¾ cup chopped onion
2 13¾-ounce cans condensed chicken broth
¾ cup chopped celery
½ cup chopped green pepper
¼ cup butter
¼ cup flour
½ teaspoon salt
¼ teaspoon ground cloves
⅛ teaspoon pepper
2 cups milk
1 cup shredded colby cheese
2½ cups cubed cooked ham
1 8-ounce can mushroom stems and pieces, drained
½ cup sliced pitted ripe olives
2 slices pasteurized processed American cheese, cut in half diagonally
  Sliced pitted ripe olives

Melt 6 tablespoons butter in a large skillet. Sauté rice and onion over medium heat, stirring frequently, until rice becomes golden brown, about 5 minutes. Stir in broth; cover. Simmer 10 minutes. Stir in celery and green pepper. Cover and simmer 10 to 15 minutes longer or until rice is tender and liquid is absorbed. Preheat oven to 350°. Meanwhile, melt ¼ cup butter in a medium-sized saucepan. Stir in flour and seasonings until smooth. Remove from heat and gradually stir in milk. Heat to boiling, stirring constantly for 1 minute. Remove from heat and stir in colby cheese until melted. If necessary, return to low heat to finish melting cheese. *Do not boil.* Combine sauce and cooked rice mixture in a large mixing bowl. Stir in ham, mushrooms and ½ cup olives. Spoon into a 2½-quart casserole. Casserole can be prepared up to this point, covered and refrigerated up to 24 hours. Bake about 20 minutes or until hot and bubbly (double baking time if refrigerated). Remove from oven and decorate top of casserole with American cheese triangles and olives. Return to oven just until cheese is melted, about 2 minutes.

Golden Pork Nuggets

Makes 6 servings.
Preparation Time: 1 hour 10 minutes.

- 2 pounds ground pork
- 1½ teaspoons salt
- ⅛ teaspoon pepper
- 6 medium-size hard-cooked eggs, peeled

Preheat oven to 375°. Sprinkle salt and pepper over ground pork. Mix lightly and divide into 6 equal portions. Form each portion into a "nest" the size of an egg. Place an egg in each and press meat around egg to cover evenly (can be refrigerated at this point until baking time). Place on rack in roasting pan. Bake 35 to 40 minutes. Serve with Sauce.

Sauce

- 2 tablespoons butter *or* margarine
- 2 tablespoons flour
- ¾ teaspoon salt
- ¼ teaspoon mace
- 2 cups milk
- 2 tablespoons chopped parsley

Melt butter; stir in flour, salt and mace. Gradually add milk and cook, stirring constantly, until thickened. Cook 5 minutes. Stir in parsley.

Tuna a la Swiss

Makes 6 servings.
Preparation Time: 45 minutes.

- 3 tablespoons margarine *or* butter
- 1 cup oven-toasted rice cereal
- ¼ cup finely chopped onion
- 1 10½-ounce can condensed cream of mushroom soup
- ⅓ cup milk
- 1 cup grated Swiss cheese
- 1½ cups cooked rice
- 1 6½-ounce can tuna, well-drained and flaked
- ¼ cup sliced stuffed green olives
- ¼ cup slivered almonds, toasted, optional
  Paprika

Preheat oven to 325°. Melt 1 tablespoon of the margarine in medium-sized frying pan over low heat. Stir in cereal, coating well. Set aside. Melt 2 tablespoons margarine in large saucepan. Add onion; sauté until tender, stirring occasionally. Add soup, milk and Swiss cheese; cook over medium heat until cheese is melted, stirring frequently. Remove from heat. Lightly stir in rice, tuna and olives. Spread mixture evenly in greased 10 x 6½ x 2-inch baking dish. Sprinkle almonds and paprika over casserole. Bake about 25 minutes or until thoroughly heated.

Cheese-Filled Shells

Makes 4 to 6 servings.
Preparation Time: 1 hour 30 minutes.

- 1 12-ounce box jumbo shells to fill (use 28 shells), cooked and drained

Filling

- 8 ounces Gruyere cheese, cubed
- 8 ounces Fontina cheese, cubed
- 1⅓ cups grated Parmesan cheese
- 1 15-ounce container ricotta cheese
- ½ teaspoon pepper

Sauce

- 2 tablespoons vegetable oil
- 1 clove garlic, minced
- ¼ cup butter *or* margarine
- ¼ cup dry bread crumbs
- 2 tablespoons chopped parsley

Preheat oven to 325°. To prepare Filling, combine Gruyere, Fontina, all but 3 tablespoons of the Parmesan, ricotta cheese and pepper. Fill each shell with 2 tablespoons of cheese mixture. Place in a 13 x 9 x 2-inch baking pan. To make Sauce, heat oil and garlic in a small saucepan. Stir in butter. Continue cooking over low heat until garlic is golden. Remove from heat. Stir in bread crumbs and parsley. Pour over shells. Sprinkle with remaining Parmesan. Cover pan. Bake 20 minutes. Remove cover. Bake an additional 10 minutes.

Shrimp Delight

Makes 6 to 8 servings.
Preparation Time: 25 minutes.

- ¼ cup butter *or* margarine
- 1 pound medium shrimp, shelled and deveined
- 1½ cups sliced mushrooms
- ½ cup sliced green onions
- 2 tablespoons chopped parsley
- ½ teaspoon salt
- ¼ teaspoon paprika
- ¼ teaspoon pepper
- 1½ cups shredded Jarlsberg cheese

Melt butter in a skillet. Sauté shrimp, mushrooms, green onions, parsley, salt, paprika and pepper until shrimp is tender. Spoon into small, individual baking dishes or a 1½-quart baking dish. Sprinkle generously with cheese. Place on a baking sheet and broil 4 inches from heat until cheese is melted. Serve immediately.

Shrimp Delight

Main Dishes

Cheesy Sausage

Makes 4 to 5 servings.
Preparation Time: 40 minutes.

- 1 pound bulk pork sausage
- 1 1-ounce package pizza-flavored Sloppy Joe mix
- 6 medium tomatoes, peeled and quartered
- ½ cup sliced Spanish olives
- 1 cup cubed Monterey Jack cheese
- Toast *or* corn bread

Brown sausage; drain fat. Add Sloppy Joe mix and tomatoes; mix well. Simmer 20 minutes, stirring occasionally. Stir in olives and cheese. Spoon mixture over squares of toast or corn bread.

Creamed Eggs

Makes 4 servings.
Preparation Time: 25 minutes.

- ¼ cup butter
- 3 tablespoons flour
- 1 teaspoon salt
- ⅛ teaspoon ground pepper
- ⅛ teaspoon paprika
- 1 teaspoon grated onion
- 2 cups milk
- 6 hard-cooked eggs, sliced *or* chopped
- 1 tablespoon finely chopped parsley
- Toast, waffles, noodles *or* corn bread

Melt butter in medium saucepan; add flour, seasonings and onion. Blend well; cook over low heat until bubbly. Add milk. Cook, stirring constantly, until thickened. Add eggs and parsley. Heat thoroughly. Adjust seasonings. Serve hot on toast or waffles, in noodle nests or over corn bread. For brunch serve over sliced tomatoes or cooked asparagus on toast.

Variations: Add 1 cup cooked vegetables *or* diced, cooked meat *or* shredded dried beef to cream sauce just before adding eggs.

Scalloped Eggs

Makes 4 servings.
Preparation Time: 20 minutes.

- 1 recipe Creamed Eggs (see above recipe)
- ½ cup fine bread crumbs
- Butter

Preheat oven to 400°. Spoon Creamed Eggs into 9-inch pie pan. Sprinkle with bread crumbs. Dot with butter. Bake until crumbs are lightly browned and sauce is bubbly, about 20 minutes.

Baked (Shirred) Eggs

Makes 4 servings.
Preparation Time: 20 minutes.

- 8 eggs
- Salt
- Pepper
- ¼ cup half-and-half *or* light cream
- 4 teaspoons butter, divided

Preheat oven to 350°. Grease four individual, shallow baking dishes. Break 2 eggs into each dish. Season with salt and pepper to taste. Spoon 1 tablespoon half-and-half over each serving. Dot each with 1 teaspoon butter. Bake until whites are set and yolks are soft and creamy, about 15 minutes. Serve immediately.

Scrambled Eggs

Makes 2 servings.
Preparation Time: 10 minutes.

- 4 eggs
- ¼ cup milk
- ½ teaspoon salt
- Dash pepper
- 2 tablespoons butter

Beat eggs, milk, salt and pepper together with a fork until well blended. Heat butter in 8-inch frypan over medium heat until just hot enough to sizzle a drop of water. Pour in egg mixture. As mixture begins to set, turn a pancake turner over and gently draw across the bottom of pan, forming large soft curds. Continue until eggs thicken, but do not stir constantly.

Note: It is better to remove scrambled eggs from pan when they are slightly underdone. Heat retained in eggs completes cooking time.

Fried Eggs

Makes 2 servings.
Preparation Time: 10 minutes.

- 1 to 2 tablespoons butter
- 4 eggs
- Salt
- Pepper

Melt butter in a frypan over medium heat until just hot enough to sizzle a drop of water. Break eggs gently into pan. Reduce heat immediately. Cook slowly to desired doneness; spoon butter over eggs to baste or turn eggs to cook both sides. Season with salt and pepper to taste.

Egg and Cheese Cakes

Makes 4 servings.
Preparation Time: 25 minutes.

    4 eggs, lightly beaten
    2 tablespoons chopped onion
    ½ cup flour
    ½ teaspoon salt
    ⅛ teaspoon pepper
    1 teaspoon baking powder
    1½ cups shredded aged Cheddar cheese
    1 tablespoon butter *or* margarine

Combine eggs with onion, flour, salt, pepper and baking powder. Stir in cheese. Heat butter on a nonstick skillet or griddle just hot enough to sizzle a drop of water. Pour ⅓-cup portions of mixture onto hot skillet. Brown well on both sides, turning once. Serve immediately with spiced fruit or other topping.

Poached Eggs

Makes 1 serving.
Preparation Time: 15 minutes.

    Oil
    Water, milk *or* broth
    Eggs, as many as desired for each serving

Lightly oil a saucepan. Add enough water to fill 2 inches deep. Heat to boiling over medium high heat. Reduce heat to keep water at a simmer. Break eggs, one at a time, into a dish. Slip each egg into water, holding dish close to water's surface. Simmer 3 to 5 minutes depending on desired doneness. When done, lift eggs with slotted pancake turner or spoon onto absorbent paper. Drain; trim edges of eggs, if desired.

Poached Eggs Florentine

Makes 6 servings.
Preparation Time: 35 minutes.

    ¼ cup butter *or* margarine
    ¼ cup flour
    ½ teaspoon salt
    ½ teaspoon liquid hot pepper sauce
    2 cups milk
    1 10-ounce package frozen chopped spinach,
      thawed, drained
    6 eggs
    3 large tomatoes, halved
      Crumbled cooked bacon
      Grated Romano cheese

Melt butter in large skillet; blend in flour, salt and hot pepper sauce; cook 2 minutes over low heat, stirring constantly. Stir in milk; cook until thick-ened, stirring constantly. Add spinach; heat to boiling. Carefully break eggs into spinach mixture; cover and cook over medium heat 5 to 8 minutes or until eggs are set. Meanwhile, broil tomato halves 3 to 5 minutes. Place an egg on each broiled tomato half; top with sauce. Serve sprinkled with bacon and Romano cheese.

Egg Fu Yong

Makes 6 patties.
Preparation Time: 25 minutes.

    1 10¾-ounce can creamy chicken-mushroom soup
    6 eggs, lightly beaten
    ¼ teaspoon salt
      Generous dash pepper
    1½ cups chopped cooked shrimp
    1 cup bean sprouts
    ½ cup chopped canned water chestnuts
    ¼ cup water
    2 teaspoons teriyaki sauce
    1 teaspoon granulated sugar
    1 teaspoon vinegar

Blend ¼ cup soup, eggs, salt and pepper in bowl. Stir in shrimp, bean sprouts and water chestnuts. For each egg fu yong patty, spoon about ¼ cup egg mixture onto hot, lightly greased griddle or skillet. Cook until golden brown on each side. Add additional oil if necessary. Drain on absorbent towels; keep warm. Combine remaining soup, water, teriyaki sauce, sugar and vinegar in saucepan. Heat thoroughly, stirring occasionally. Serve with egg fu yong.

Eggs Benedict with Stuffing

Makes 6 servings.
Preparation Time: 40 minutes.

    1 6-ounce package stuffing mix, any flavor
    ¼ cup butter *or* margarine, melted
      Nonstick vegetable spray
    1½ cups hot water
    1¼ cups slivered cooked ham
    6 eggs

Preheat oven to 400°. Combine contents of vegetable/seasoning packet of stuffing mix, butter and water in a 8½ x 11 x 2-inch pan that has been sprayed with a nonstick vegetable spray. Stir to blend. Add stuffing; stir until just moistened. Spread evenly in dish and sprinkle ham over stuffing. Divide into 6 squares. Make a depression in center of each stuffing square and carefully break 1 egg into each. Bake 20 minutes or until eggs are set and cooked.

Soufflés

Basic Soufflé

Makes 2 to 4 servings.
Preparation Time: 1 hour.

 ¼ cup butter
 ¼ cup flour
 ½ teaspoon salt
 1 cup milk
 4 eggs, separated
 ½ teaspoon cream of tartar
   Seasoning, optional

Preheat oven to 350°. Melt butter in medium saucepan over medium-high heat. Blend in flour and salt. Cook, stirring constantly, until mixture is smooth and bubbly. Stir in milk all at once. Cook and stir until mixture boils and is smooth and thickened. Set aside. Beat egg whites in large bowl with cream of tartar at high speed until stiff but not dry. Blend egg yolks thoroughly into sauce; add seasoning, if desired. Fold sauce mixture gently, but thoroughly, into whites. Pour carefully into 1½- to 2-quart soufflé dish. Bake until puffy, delicately browned, and soufflé shakes slightly when oven rack is gently moved back and forth, about 30 to 40 minutes. Serve immediately.

Note: For a soufflé to serve 4 to 6, use:

 ⅓ cup butter
 ⅓ cup flour
 ¾ teaspoon salt
 1½ cups milk
 6 eggs, separated
 ¾ teaspoon cream of tartar
   Seasoning, optional

Bake in 2- to 2½-quart soufflé dish, about 35 to 45 minutes.

Savory Soufflé Variations

To use with Basic Soufflé

After sauce has thickened, stir in:

Carrot: 1 cup shredded, cooked carrot, ½ cup shredded Cheddar cheese and ½ teaspoon dried dillweed.

Cheese: 1 cup shredded Cheddar, Swiss *or* mozzarella cheese and ½ teaspoon dry mustard.

Corn-Cheddar: 1 7-ounce can whole kernel corn, well drained (use liquid in place of some of the milk), ½ cup shredded Cheddar *or* Monterey Jack cheese and 1 teaspoon dry minced onion.

Cheese Soufflé

Makes 4 to 6 servings.
Preparation Time: 1 hour 30 minutes.

 ¼ cup quick-cooking tapioca
 ½ teaspoon salt
 1 cup milk
 1 cup shredded mild Cheddar cheese
 4 eggs, separated

Preheat oven to 350°. Combine tapioca, salt and milk in saucepan; let stand 5 minutes. Cook and stir over medium heat until mixture comes to a boil. Remove from heat. Add cheese, stirring until melted. Cool slightly. Beat egg whites until stiff but not dry. Beat egg yolks until thickened and light in color; beat in tapioca mixture. Fold into beaten egg whites. Pour into 1½-quart baking dish. Place dish in pan of hot water in oven. Bake 50 to 55 minutes or until firm.

Asparagus Soufflé

Makes 6 servings.
Preparation Time: 1 hour 20 minutes.

 ¼ cup butter *or* margarine
 ¼ cup flour
 1⅓ cups warm milk
 ¼ cup grated aged American cheese
 5 eggs, separated
 ½ teaspoon salt
 ⅛ teaspoon garlic salt
 1 pound fresh asparagus cooked and chopped *or*
   1 10-ounce package frozen asparagus cuts
   and tips, cooked according to package directions
 ½ teaspoon salt

Preheat oven to 350°. Melt butter, add flour and mix into a smooth paste. Add milk slowly and cook over low heat until thickened, stirring constantly. Add cheese and cook only until melted. Remove from heat. Add well beaten egg yolks with ½ teaspoon salt to cheese mixture. Add garlic salt and asparagus. Sprinkle egg whites with ½ teaspoon salt and beat until stiff. Fold in cheese mixture and mix only until well blended. Bake 60 minutes in well-greased 1½-quart soufflé dish placed in a larger pan with 1 inch hot water.

Frozen Strawberry Soufflé, page 37

Soufflés

Soufflé Italian

Makes 4 to 5 servings.
Preparation Time: 1 hour 10 minutes.

- 3 tablespoons butter
- 3 tablespoons grated Parmesan cheese
- 1 clove garlic, minced
- 1 cup chopped green onion
- 1 cup shredded zucchini
- 4 eggs, separated
- 1 8-ounce carton ricotta cheese
- ¼ cup sour half-and-half
- ½ teaspoon crushed tarragon
- ½ teaspoon salt
- ¼ teaspoon ground nutmeg
- 1 15½-ounce can pink salmon, drained and skin removed
- ¼ teaspoon cream of tartar

Preheat oven to 350°. Coat inside of a 1-quart soufflé dish with 1 tablespoon of butter. Sprinkle with grated Parmesan cheese. Heat remaining 2 tablespoons butter in skillet. Add garlic, onion and zucchini; sauté until vegetables are just tender. Remove vegetables from skillet and set aside. In the same skillet, combine egg yolks, ricotta cheese, sour half-and-half, tarragon, salt and nutmeg. Cook over low heat, stirring constantly, until sauce thickens. Remove from heat. Stir sautéed vegetables into sauce. Fold in salmon. Beat egg whites until foamy. Add cream of tartar and beat until egg whites are stiff but not dry. Fold one-fourth of egg whites into salmon mixture. Gently fold in remaining egg whites. Spoon into prepared soufflé dish. Bake 45 minutes. Serve immediately.

Cold Lemon Soufflé

Makes 6 to 8 servings.
Preparation Time: 20 minutes; chill overnight.

- 1 envelope unflavored gelatin
- 1 tablespoon milk, warmed
- 3 eggs, separated
  Juice from 3 lemons *or* ½ cup reconstituted lemon juice
- 1½ tablespoons grated lemon rind
- ¾ cup granulated sugar
- 1¼ cups whipping cream, whipped

Stir gelatin into warm milk until dissolved. Combine egg yolks, lemon juice, lemon rind, sugar and gelatin mixture in the top of a double boiler. Heat, stirring until thickened. Cool pan in bowl of ice, stirring occasionally. Beat egg whites until stiff. Whip cream. Fold egg whites and whipped

cream into thickened lemon mixture. Spoon into soufflé dish and chill overnight. Serve cold.

Hot Chocolate Soufflé

Makes 4 to 6 servings.
Preparation Time: 1 hour.

- ½ cup granulated sugar, divided
- ⅓ cup unsweetened cocoa
- ¼ cup flour
- ⅛ teaspoon salt
- 1 cup milk
- ½ teaspoon vanilla
- 4 eggs, separated
- ½ teaspoon cream of tartar

Preheat oven to 350°. Combine ¼ cup of the sugar, cocoa, flour and salt in medium saucepan. Stir in milk. Cook over medium heat, stirring constantly, until mixture boils and is smooth and thickened. Stir in vanilla. Set aside. Beat egg whites with cream of tartar in large bowl at high speed until foamy. Add remaining ¼ cup sugar, 2 tablespoons at a time, beating constantly until sugar is dissolved and whites are glossy and stand in soft peaks. Blend egg yolks thoroughly into reserved sauce. Fold yolk mixture into whites gently, but thoroughly. Carefully pour into 1½- to 2-quart soufflé dish. Bake 30 to 40 minutes until puffy, delicately browned and soufflé shakes slightly when oven rack is moved gently back and forth. Serve immediately.

Plum Soufflé

Makes 4 to 6 servings.
Preparation Time: 40 minutes; 3 hours or overnight to chill.

- 6 large blue plums, pitted and diced
- ½ cup granulated sugar
- 1½ cups water
- 3 envelopes unflavored gelatin
- 5 egg whites
  Whipped cream to garnish
- 1 large blue plum, sliced to garnish

Prepare a 3-cup soufflé dish by fastening a 2-inch aluminum foil collar with tape or string around the top of dish. Combine plums, sugar and 1 cup of water in saucepan. Cover and simmer until plums are soft. Remove from heat. Force plums through sieve. Combine gelatin and remaining water in saucepan. Cook over low heat, stirring constantly, until gelatin is dissolved. Stir in plum purée. Remove from heat and cool thoroughly. Beat egg whites with electric mixer until stiff peaks form. Gently fold whites into plum mixture. Carefully pour soufflé into prepared dish. Refrigerate until firm, at least 3 hours. Serve garnished with whipped cream and sliced plums.

Frozen Strawberry Soufflé

Makes 6 servings.
Preparation Time: 1 hour 15 minutes; chill overnight.

  Butter
  Granulated sugar
1 envelope unflavored gelatin
1 cup granulated sugar, divided
¾ cup cold water
3 cups fresh strawberries, washed and hulled
4 eggs, separated
¼ teaspoon cream of tartar
  Red food coloring, optional
1 cup whipping cream, whipped

Butter bottom and sides of 1½-quart soufflé dish; sprinkle with sugar. Make a 4-inch band of aluminum foil, triple thickness, long enough to wrap around dish and overlap 2 inches. Lightly butter inside of band and sprinkle with sugar. Fasten with tape, paper clip or string; collar should extend 2 inches above rim of dish. Combine gelatin and ¾ cup of the sugar in medium saucepan. Stir in water and let stand 1 minute. Cook, stirring constantly, over low heat until gelatin dissolves completely, 5 to 8 minutes. Remove from heat. Mash strawberries; blend into gelatin mixture. Beat egg yolks at high speed in small bowl until thickened and lemon-colored, about 5 minutes. Blend a little of hot gelatin mixture into yolks. Blend yolk mixture into gelatin mixture in saucepan. Chill, stirring occasionally, until mixture mounds slightly when dropped from a spoon, 30 to 45 minutes. Wash and dry beaters. Beat egg whites and cream of tartar in large bowl at high speed until foamy. Add remaining ¼ cup sugar, 1 tablespoon at a time, beating constantly until sugar is dissolved and whites are glossy and stand in soft peaks. Beat in few drops of food coloring, if desired. Fold chilled gelatin mixture and whipped cream gently but thoroughly into egg whites. Carefully pour into prepared dish. Chill overnight until firm. Just before serving, carefully remove foil band.

Brandy Alexander Soufflé

Makes 6 servings.
Preparation Time: 1 hour 15 minutes; chill overnight.

  Butter
  Granulated sugar
  Shaved chocolate
½ cup granulated sugar, divided
1½ envelopes unflavored gelatin
½ cup water
6 eggs, separated
2 3-ounce packages cream cheese, softened
⅓ cup brandy
⅓ cup creme de cacao
¼ teaspoon cream of tartar
2 cups whipping cream
  Chocolate curls, optional

Butter bottom and sides of 1½-quart soufflé dish; sprinkle with sugar. Make 4-inch band of aluminum foil, triple thickness, long enough to wrap around dish and overlap 2 inches. Butter inside of band and sprinkle with shaved chocolate. Fasten with tape, paper clip or string; collar should extend 2 inches above rim of dish. Combine ¼ cup sugar and gelatin in medium saucepan. Stir in water and let stand 1 minute. Cook, stirring constantly, over low heat until gelatin dissolves, 5 to 8 minutes. Remove from heat. Beat egg yolks in small bowl at high speed until thickened and lemon-colored, about 5 minutes. Blend a little of hot gelatin mixture into yolks. Blend yolk mixture into gelatin mixture in saucepan. Cook, stirring constantly, over low heat 2 to 3 minutes. Remove from heat. Blend in cream cheese, brandy and creme de cacao. Chill, stirring occasionally, until mixture mounds slightly when dropped from a spoon, 30 to 45 minutes. Wash and dry beaters. Beat egg whites and cream of tartar at high speed until foamy. Add remaining ¼ cup sugar, 1 tablespoon at a time, beating constantly until sugar is dissolved and whites are glossy and stand in soft peaks. Set aside. Beat 1½ cups whipping cream until stiff. (Reserve remaining ½ cup cream.) Fold cream cheese mixture and whipped cream gently but thoroughly into egg whites. Pour into prepared dish. Chill overnight until firm. Just before serving, carefully remove foil band. Garnish soufflé with chocolate curls, if desired. Whip remaining cream until stiff. Serve with soufflé.

Quiches

Sausage Quiche

Makes 6 to 8 servings.
Preparation Time: 1 hour.

1½ cups flour
½ teaspoon salt
½ cup shortening
1 egg, separated
¼ cup water
½ pound bulk pork sausage
¼ cup minced onion
1 cup shredded Swiss cheese
4 eggs
2 cups milk
½ teaspoon salt
Dash cayenne pepper

Preheat oven to 375°. Stir flour and ½ teaspoon salt together. Cut shortening into flour until pieces are size of small peas. Beat egg yolk with water. Sprinkle into flour mixture a little at a time, mixing lightly until dough begins to stick together. If necessary, add more water. Press together. Turn out onto lightly floured surface and roll into circle ⅛ inch thick. Gently fit into ungreased 9-inch pie pan. Trim pastry and flute edge of dough; brush pastry with lightly beaten egg white. Fry sausage and onion; drain. Sprinkle sausage, onion and cheese in unbaked pie shell. Beat together 4 eggs, milk, ½ teaspoon salt and pepper; pour into pie shell. Bake 30 to 40 minutes or until knife inserted in center comes out clean. Cool slightly before serving.

Salmon Quiche

Makes 6 to 8 servings.
Preparation Time: 1 hour 20 minutes.

1 unbaked 10-inch pastry shell
1 9-ounce package frozen chopped spinach, cooked and drained
1½ cups shredded Monterey Jack cheese
1 3-ounce package cream cheese, softened
½ teaspoon salt
½ teaspoon thyme
1 15½-ounce can pink salmon, drained and flaked
4 eggs, lightly beaten
1 cup milk

Preheat oven to 375°. Bake pastry shell 10 minutes. Combine spinach, cheeses, salt and thyme. Sprinkle salmon evenly in pastry shell. Spoon spinach mixture into pastry shell. Combine eggs and milk; pour into pastry shell. Bake 40 to 45 minutes. Let stand 10 minutes before serving.

Broccoli-Chicken Quiche

Makes 4 servings.
Preparation Time: 1 hour 30 minutes.

1 unbaked 9-inch pastry shell, chilled
1 cup shredded Swiss cheese
1 10-ounce package frozen, chopped broccoli, cooked, drained and cooled
1 chicken breast, cooked, skinned, boned, and diced
4 green onions including tops, diced
3 eggs, lightly beaten
1 cup half-and-half
½ cup milk
½ teaspoon seasoned salt
⅛ teaspoon salt
Dash white pepper
¼ cup grated Parmesan cheese

Preheat oven to 375°. Sprinkle Swiss cheese over the bottom of the chilled pastry crust. Sprinkle with broccoli, diced chicken and green onions. Combine eggs, half-and-half, milk and seasonings; blend well; pour into pastry shell. Sprinkle with Parmesan cheese. Bake 40 to 45 minutes or until knife inserted in center comes out clean. Let stand 5 minutes before serving.

Note: 1 cup diced, cooked turkey can be substituted for the chicken.

Quiche Lorraine

Makes 6 servings.
Preparation Time: 1 hour 15 minutes.

1 unbaked 9-inch pastry shell
6 eggs, lightly beaten
8 slices bacon, cooked, drained and crumbled
1 cup shredded Swiss cheese
1¼ cups half-and-half *or* milk
½ teaspoon salt
⅛ teaspoon ground nutmeg
⅛ teaspoon white pepper

Preheat oven to 450°. Brush pastry shell with a small amount of beaten egg. Prick bottom and sides of pastry shell with fork. Bake the shell until golden brown, about 5 minutes. Cool on wire rack. Sprinkle bacon and cheese in pastry shell. Combine remaining ingredients and beat until thoroughly blended. Pour into pastry shell. Reduce oven temperature to 375°. Bake for 35 to 40 minutes or until knife inserted in center comes out clean. Let stand 5 minutes before serving.

Quiches

Onion and Bacon Quiche

Makes 6 to 8 servings.
Preparation Time: 1 hour 25 minutes.

1 unbaked 9-inch pastry shell
1 cup chopped onion
¼ cup butter
2 tablespoons flour
⅓ cup cooking sherry
1 pint dairy sour cream
3 eggs, lightly beaten
4 slices crisp cooked bacon, crumbled
3 tablespoons chopped parsley
1 teaspoon Worcestershire sauce
1 teaspoon celery seed
¼ teaspoon paprika
½ teaspoon salt
　Dash white pepper
¼ cup grated Parmesan cheese
　Paprika

Preheat oven to 350°. Cook onion in butter in large skillet over low heat for 10 minutes, stirring frequently. Stir in flour, mixing well; add sherry. Remove from heat. Blend sour cream into eggs; stir in bacon, parsley, Worcestershire sauce, celery seed, paprika, salt and pepper. Pour into onion mixture and blend well. Pour into pastry shell. Sprinkle with Parmesan cheese and paprika. Bake 40 to 45 minutes or until filling is set. Let stand 15 minutes before serving.

Mushroom Quiche

Makes 6 servings.
Preparation Time: 1 hour 10 minutes.

1 baked 9-inch pastry shell
½ pound fresh mushrooms, sliced
¼ cup sliced green onions, including tops
1 tablespoon butter
1 cup shredded Swiss cheese
4 eggs
1 cup milk
¼ cup grated Parmesan cheese
½ teaspoon salt
⅛ teaspoon pepper

Preheat oven to 375°. Cook mushrooms and onions in butter in large skillet over medium heat until mushrooms are lightly browned, 6 to 8 minutes. Spread mushroom mixture evenly in pastry shell; sprinkle Swiss cheese over mushroom mixture. Beat remaining ingredients together until well blended. Pour into pastry shell. Bake 30 to 40 minutes or until knife inserted in center comes out clean. Let stand 5 minutes before serving.

Hot Quiche Squares

Makes 9 servings.
Preparation Time: 50 minutes.

4 eggs
¼ cup flour
½ teaspoon baking powder
½ teaspoon salt
1 12-ounce can whole kernel golden corn, drained
10 ounces Monterey Jack cheese, shredded
¾ cup cottage cheese
1 2-ounce jar sliced pimientos, drained and chopped
⅓ cup chopped onion
¼ cup chopped pickled jalapeno pepper strips

Preheat oven to 350°. Beat eggs for 1 minute. Combine flour, baking powder and salt; add to eggs and mix well. Stir in remaining ingredients. Pour into an 8-inch square baking dish. Bake uncovered 30 to 35 minutes or until knife inserted in center comes out clean.

Tuna, Mushroom and Tomato Quiche

Makes 6 servings.
Preparation Time: 1 hour 15 minutes.

　Pastry for 1 10-inch piecrust
　Uncooked rice
4 eggs
1 tablespoon butter or margarine
¼ pound fresh mushrooms, sliced or 1 4-ounce can sliced mushrooms, drained
1 7-ounce can tuna in oil, drained
1 large tomato, peeled and sliced
1¾ cups milk
1 cup grated Swiss cheese
½ cup grated Gruyere cheese
¾ teaspoon salt
½ teaspoon paprika
¾ teaspoon grated onion

Preheat oven to 425°. Line a 10-inch quiche pan or pie plate with pastry, making sure that the crust is 2 inches higher than top of pan. Prick holes in the bottom of shell with fork; line bottom with waxed paper. Spread a generous amount of uncooked rice over waxed paper and bake 5 minutes. Remove rice and waxed paper from shell and discard; bake an additional 5 minutes. Cool; brush with 1 lightly beaten egg white; set aside. Reduce heat to 325°. If using fresh mushrooms melt butter in a skillet; add mushrooms; cook just until tender. Layer mushrooms, tuna and tomato in pastry shell. Heat milk in a saucepan, add grated cheeses and stir until melted. Add salt, paprika and onion. Remove from heat and beat in remaining 3 eggs and egg yolk 1 at a time. Pour mixture into pastry shell; bake for 45 minutes until custard is set.

Ham-Asparagus Quiche

Makes 6 servings.
Preparation Time: 30 minutes.

    1 unbaked 9-inch pastry shell
    1 cup diced, cooked ham
    1 10-ounce package frozen asparagus spears, thawed
    1 cup cubed Cheddar *or* Swiss cheese
    ¼ cup finely chopped onion
    ¼ teaspoon salt
    3 eggs, lightly beaten
    1 cup milk

Preheat oven to 400°. Layer ingredients in the pastry shell in the order given. Combine the eggs and milk; pour into pastry shell. Bake 10 minutes. Reduce heat to 350° and bake 25 minutes.

Beefy Quiche

Makes 6 servings.
Preparation Time: 1 hour.

    1 baked 9-inch pie shell
    1 pound ground beef
    ½ cup chopped onion *or* 2 tablespoons instant minced onion
    6 eggs
    1 10¾-ounce can condensed cream of tomato soup, undiluted

Preheat oven to 375°. Cook ground beef with onion in large skillet over medium heat until beef is lightly browned. Drain well; sprinkle into pie shell. Beat eggs and soup together until well blended. Pour over beef mixture. Bake 30 to 40 minutes until knife inserted in center comes out clean. Let stand 5 minutes before serving.

Quiche Americaine

Makes 6 servings.
Preparation Time: 1 hour.

    1 baked 9-inch pastry shell
    1 cup shredded Swiss cheese
    ½ cup chopped cooked chicken *or* 1 5-ounce can boned chicken
    6 eggs
    1½ cups milk
    1 teaspoon poultry seasoning
    1 teaspoon salt

Preheat oven to 375°. Sprinkle cheese and chicken into pastry shell. Beat remaining ingre-

dients together until well blended. Pour into pastry shell. Bake 30 to 40 minutes or until knife inserted in center comes out clean. Let stand 5 minutes before serving.

Crustless Carrot Quiche

Makes 6 servings.
Preparation Time: 1 hour.

    2 cups finely shredded carrots
    6 eggs
    1¼ cups skim milk
    1 tablespoon dry minced onion
    ½ teaspoon salt
    ¼ teaspoon ground ginger
    ⅛ teaspoon pepper
    1 cup shredded Cheddar cheese

Preheat oven to 350°. Heat 1-inch water to boiling point in medium saucepan. Add carrots. Cover, reduce heat and simmer until tender, about 5 minutes. Drain in colander, pressing out water. Beat eggs, milk, onion, salt, ginger and pepper together until well blended. Stir in drained carrots and cheese. Pour into buttered 9-inch quiche pan. Set pan in large baking pan. Place on rack in oven. Pour hot water into baking pan to within ½ inch of top of quiche pan. Bake 30 to 35 minutes or until knife inserted in center comes out clean. Let stand 5 minutes before serving.

Quick Tuna Quiche

Makes 6 servings.
Preparation Time: 1 hour 15 minutes.

    1 unbaked 9-inch pastry shell
    1 cup milk
    ½ cup mayonnaise
    2 eggs, lightly beaten
    1 tablespoon cornstarch
    1 7-ounce can tuna, drained and flaked
    ½ pound Cheddar cheese, cubed
    ⅓ cup chopped green onions
    1 teaspoon Dijon mustard
    ½ teaspoon salt
    ½ teaspoon Worcestershire sauce

Preheat oven to 350°. Stir milk, mayonnaise, eggs and cornstarch together in medium bowl until smooth. Stir in tuna, cheese, onions, mustard, salt and Worcestershire sauce. Pour into pastry shell. Bake for 45 minutes, or until knife inserted in center comes out clean.

Omelets & Pancakes

Basic Omelet

Makes 1 serving.
Preparation Time: 15 minutes.

    2 to 3 eggs
    2 to 3 tablespoons water
    ⅛ to ¼ teaspoon salt
       Dash pepper
    1 tablespoon butter

Mix eggs, water, salt and pepper until blended. Heat butter in 7- to 10-inch omelet pan or skillet over medium-high heat until just hot enough to sizzle a drop of water. Pour in egg mixture. Mixture should immediately set at edge. With an inverted pancake turner, carefully push cooked portion at edge toward center so uncooked portion can reach hot pan surface, tilting pan as necessary. While top is still moist and creamy, fill if desired with one or more Omelet Fillings. With pancake turner, fold omelet in half or roll, and invert onto plate with a quick flip of the wrist or slide from pan onto plate. It is better to fill omelet when it is slightly underdone; heat retained in eggs completes the cooking.

Omelet Fillings

       Cheese, shredded
       Salami, diced
       Green pepper, diced
       Onion, diced
       Mushrooms, sliced
       Ham, diced
       Tomato, diced

Choose any of the above fillings or a combination thereof for a perfect complement to a puffy, tender omelet.

Omelet Delight

Makes 4 to 6 servings.
Preparation Time: 15 minutes.

    1 cup hard salami, cut into strips
    ¼ cup sliced green onions
    2 tablespoons butter *or* margarine
    5 eggs
    ¼ cup water
    1 teaspoon salt
    ⅛ teaspoon pepper
    1 cup shredded Jarlsberg cheese

Sauté salami and onions in butter in large skillet; cook until onion is translucent. Beat eggs, water, salt and pepper until blended. Pour into skillet. Cook over low heat until set. Sprinkle cheese over surface of omelet. Cover and cook until cheese is melted and omelet is puffed.

Zucchini Omelet

Makes 6 servings.
Preparation Time: 50 minutes.

    1 11-inch zucchini, thinly sliced
    3 medium tomatoes, peeled and quartered
    1 slice bacon, diced
    4 eggs, beaten
    ¾ cup shredded Monterey Jack cheese
    ¼ cup milk
    ½ teaspoon salt
    1 tablespoon chopped parsley
    2 teaspoons cornstarch
    ¼ cup sliced ripe olives

Sauté zucchini and tomatoes in medium saucepan until zucchini is tender, about 10 minutes. Drain zucchini, reserving tomato sauce. Cook bacon until crisp in 10-inch skillet. Add zucchini. Combine eggs, cheese, milk, salt and parsley. Pour over zucchini and bacon. Cover and cook over low heat 15 minutes. Dissolve cornstarch in reserved sauce in saucepan. Cook, stirring constantly, until thickened. Add olives. Cut omelet into wedges. Serve with sauce.

Herbed-Cheese Omelet

Makes 1 serving.
Preparation Time: 20 minutes.

    ½ cup cottage cheese
    1 tablespoon chopped chives *or* snipped parsley
    2 eggs
    2 tablespoons water
    ⅛ teaspoon crushed basil
       Dash pepper
    1 tablespoon butter

Combine cheese and chives; set aside. Beat eggs, water, basil and pepper until blended. Heat butter in 8-inch skillet until just hot enough to sizzle a drop of water. Pour in egg mixture. Mixture should set at edge at once. Carefully draw cooked portions at edge toward center with pancake turner so uncooked portion flows underneath, tilting pan if necessary. Slide pan rapidly back and forth over heat to keep mixture in motion. While top is still moist, place cottage cheese mixture on half of omelet. With pancake turner fold in half or roll, turning out onto plate with a quick flip of the wrist. Serve at once.

Omelets & Pancakes

Puffy Apple Omelet

Makes 2 servings.
Preparation Time: 35 minutes.

  2 tart unpeeled apples, sliced
  3 tablespoons butter
  2 tablespoons brown sugar
  ½ teaspoon grated orange peel
  ⅛ teaspoon cinnamon
  4 eggs, separated
  ¼ cup water
  ¼ teaspoon cream of tartar
  1 tablespoon granulated sugar

Preheat oven to 350°. In small saucepan combine apple slices, 2 tablespoons of the butter, brown sugar, orange peel and cinnamon. Cook over medium heat, gently turning apple slices until tender and glazed, about 5 minutes; keep warm while preparing omelet. Beat egg whites, water and cream of tartar in large bowl until foamy. Add sugar, beating constantly until sugar is dissolved (rub a bit of mixture between thumb and forefinger to feel if sugar is dissolved) and whites are glossy and form soft peaks. Beat egg yolks in small bowl at high speed until thick and lemon-colored. Gently but thoroughly fold yolks into whites. Heat the remaining 1 tablespoon butter in a 10-inch ovenproof skillet over medium-high heat until just hot enough to sizzle a drop of water. Pour in omelet mixture. Gently smooth surface. Reduce heat to medium and cook until puffy and lightly browned, 3 to 5 minutes. Lift omelet at edge to check color. Place skillet in oven and bake until knife inserted halfway between center and outside edge comes out clean, 10 to 12 minutes. To serve: loosen omelet edge with spatula. Cut through center of omelet with a sharp knife but *do not* cut through to bottom. Spoon warm apples over half of omelet. With pancake turner, fold omelet in half and slide onto platter. Serve immediately.

Basic Crepes

Makes 16.
Preparation Time: 2 hours 25 minutes.

  3 eggs, beaten
 1⅓ cups milk
  3 tablespoons butter, melted
  1 cup flour
  ½ teaspoon salt

Combine eggs, milk and butter; beat well. Combine flour and salt. Gradually add flour mixture to egg mixture. Beat until smooth. Chill at least 2 hours. Heat greased 6-inch skillet until a drop of water sizzles. Place 2 tablespoons batter into skillet; rotate so batter covers bottom completely. Cook over medium to medium-high heat for about 1 minute. When brown, turn to brown other side. Cook about 30 seconds to 1 minute. Repeat for each crepe. Stack crepes on ovenproof plate or baking dish and keep in warm oven until all are ready to be filled.

Cheese-Stuffed Crepes

Makes 5 to 6 servings.
Preparation Time: 1 hour.

 15 to 18 Basic Crepes (Recipe on this page)
    Ricotta Filling
  2 8-ounce cans tomato sauce
  1 cup shredded mozzarella cheese
  ¼ cup grated Parmesan cheese

Preheat oven to 400°. Make crepes. Prepare Ricotta Filling. Place 2 to 3 tablespoons filling on each crepe; roll jelly-roll fashion. Place crepes in large shallow baking dish. Cover with tomato sauce; sprinkle with mozzarella and Parmesan cheeses. Bake 15 minutes or until thoroughly heated.

Ricotta Filling

  1 pound ricotta cheese
  ½ cup grated Parmesan cheese
  ½ cup chopped cooked fresh *or* frozen chopped
    spinach, thawed
  1 teaspoon seasoned salt
  ⅛ teaspoon white pepper
  3 eggs, beaten

Blend ingredients together.

Strawberry Creme Crepes

Makes 6 to 8 servings.
Preparation Time: 45 minutes.

 18 to 20 Basic Crepes (Recipe on this page)
  ½ cup granulated sugar
  1 pint fresh strawberries, sliced
  1 8-ounce package cream cheese, softened
  ¼ cup confectioners' sugar

Prepare crepes. Sprinkle granulated sugar over 1 cup of the strawberries; set aside. Combine cream cheese and sugar. Blend remaining 1 cup of the berries into cheese mixture. Spread about 1 tablespoon filling on each crepe; roll up. Serve with reserved sweetened strawberries.

Buttermilk Pancakes

Makes 16 4-inch pancakes.
Preparation Time: 30 minutes.

- **3 eggs, room temperature, separated**
- **1⅔ cups buttermilk**
- **1 teaspoon baking soda**
- **1½ cups flour**
- **1 tablespoon granulated sugar**
- **1½ teaspoons baking powder**
- **¾ teaspoon salt**
- **3 tablespoons butter, melted**

Preheat griddle over medium heat. Beat egg yolks in medium bowl until thickened. Combine buttermilk and baking soda. Add to egg yolks. Blend well. Combine dry ingredients. Blend into yolk mixture. Stir in melted butter. Beat egg whites until stiff peaks form. Gently fold into batter. Pour batter onto preheated griddle, using ¼ cup of batter at a time. Cook until pancakes are puffed and surface bubbles. Before bubbles break, turn and brown on other side.

Note: If pancake batter will stand a long time prior to cooking, add a little extra baking powder to batter. Keep pancakes warm in a low oven while cooking rest of batter.

Cheesy Pancake Rolls

Makes 15.
Preparation Time: 1 hour 10 minutes.

- **4 eggs**
- **1 cup flour**
- **¼ teaspoon salt**
- **1½ cups milk**
- **3 tablespoons butter, melted**
- **4 cups ricotta cheese**
- **½ cup grated fresh Parmesan cheese**
- **¼ cup chopped parsley**
- **½ cup seedless raisins**
- **¼ cup finely crushed walnuts**
- **1 teaspoon salt**
- **⅛ teaspoon black pepper**
- **½ teaspoon ground nutmeg**
-   **Melted butter**

Preheat oven to 350°. Beat 3 eggs lightly in small bowl. Add flour and salt; beat until smooth and thickened. Gradually add milk; blend until smooth. Add 3 tablespoons melted butter; blend well. Set aside while making cheese filling. Beat remaining egg in medium bowl. Add ricotta and Parmesan cheese and remaining ingredients, except melted butter. Blend well and set filling aside. Heat a 6-inch nonstick skillet over medium heat. Stir batter and pour ¼ cup batter into

skillet. Tilt pan at once to form even circle. Brown on both sides, being careful not to tear pancake when turning. Place pancake on waxed paper when done. Cool slightly. Place ¼ cup cheese filling in center of each pancake. Spread filling evenly over pancake. Roll up jelly-roll fashion and place seam-side down on lightly greased ovenproof baking dish. Brush tops with melted butter*. Bake 15 to 20 minutes or until well heated. Serve with favorite fruit sauce.

Note: Pancakes can be made ahead to this point, covered and refrigerated until just before baking.

Swiss Cheese Pancakes

Makes 24 3-inch pancakes.
Preparation Time: 30 minutes.

- **¾ cup dairy sour cream**
- **3 egg yolks, lightly beaten**
- **6 ounces Swiss cheese, grated**
- **2 tablespoons plus 1 teaspoon flour**
- **¾ teaspoon salt**
-   **Few grains pepper**
- **1½ teaspoons thyme**
- **½ teaspoon dry mustard**
- **2 tablespoons butter**

Add sour cream and egg yolks to cheese; mix well. Mix the flour, salt, pepper, thyme and mustard together; blend into cheese mixture. Melt butter in a heavy skillet. Drop batter by teaspoonfuls into skillet. Cook over medium heat until lightly browned on bottom. Loosen edge with a spatula; turn and lightly brown other side.

Potato Pancakes

Makes 24 3-inch pancakes.
Preparation Time: 45 minutes.

- **1 cup ricotta cheese** *or* **pot cheese**
- **1 egg**
- **2 tablespoons flour**
- **1¾ cups pared and shredded potatoes**
- **1 cup chopped ham**
- **1 6-ounce can sliced mushrooms, drained**

Preheat nonstick skillet. Combine ricotta cheese, egg and flour in large bowl; blend well. Stir in potatoes, ham and mushrooms. Drop heaping tablespoons of potato mixture onto skillet. Brown pancakes over medium heat on one side about 3 minutes; turn and brown other side. Repeat with remaining batter. Serve warm.

Sandwiches & Breads

Beef Puff

Makes 4 servings.
Preparation Time: 2 hours 10 minutes.

- 2 cups ground *or* chopped cooked beef
- ½ cup mayonnaise
- 2 tablespoons snipped parsley
- 1 teaspoon salt
- ⅛ teaspoon pepper
- 8 slices bread
  Butter *or* margarine, softened
- 3 eggs, beaten
- 2 cups milk
- ¼ teaspoon salt
- ¼ teaspoon sage
  Paprika, optional

Combine beef, mayonnaise, parsley, 1 teaspoon salt and pepper. Spread 4 slices bread with butter, and divide meat mixture into 4 equal portions. Place 1 portion on each slice of bread and top with a slice of bread. Place sandwiches in greased 9 x 9-inch baking pan. Combine eggs, milk, ¼ teaspoon salt and sage; mix well. Pour over sandwiches, sprinkle with paprika and let stand in refrigerator at least 1 hour. Bake at 350° 45 to 50 minutes or until puffed and golden.

Ham Sandwich Bake

Makes 6 servings.
Preparation Time: 3 hours 15 minutes.

- 1½ pounds cooked smoked ham
  Nonstick vegetable spray
- 12 slices white bread
- 6 1-ounce slices Swiss cheese
- ¼ cup mayonnaise
- 1 tablespoon prepared mustard
- 1 teaspoon caraway seed
- 4 eggs
- 3 cups milk
- ½ teaspoon salt

Cut ham in ⅛- to ¼-inch thick slices. Spray a 13 x 9-inch baking pan with nonstick vegetable spray; place 6 slices of bread in pan. Top each slice of bread with a slice of cheese and pieces of ham. Combine mayonnaise, mustard and caraway seed; spread on remaining 6 slices of bread and place, spread side down, on ham. Beat eggs, milk and salt together until foamy; pour over sandwiches. Cover pan; refrigerate 2 hours. Bake 1 hour at 325°.

Mexican Egg Salad Sandwiches

Makes 6.
Preparation Time: 30 minutes.

- ⅓ cup dairy sour cream
- 3 tablespoons chopped, drained green chilies
- 1 tablespoon lemon juice
- 1 teaspoon salt
- 1 to 2 teaspoons bottled taco sauce
- 9 hard-cooked eggs, chopped
- 6 slices tomato
- 6 slices bread, toasted *or* 6 corn tortillas, warmed
- ½ cup shredded Cheddar cheese

Blend sour cream, chilies, lemon juice, salt and taco sauce together. Stir in eggs. Place 1 tomato slice on 1 toast slice for each sandwich. Spread ⅓ cup egg salad on each tomato slice; sprinkle with 1 rounded tablespoon cheese. Broil 4 inches from heat just until cheese melts, 2 to 3 minutes.

Turkey Pizza Burgers

Makes 8.
Preparation Time: 25 minutes.

- 3 tablespoons butter
- 1 cup diced celery
- 3 cups finely chopped cooked turkey
- 1 8-ounce can tomato sauce
- 1 teaspoon salt
- 1 teaspoon ground oregano
- ½ teaspoon pepper
- 4 hamburger buns, halved, toasted and buttered
- 8 1-ounce slices Provolone cheese

Preheat oven to 300°. Melt butter in large skillet. Sauté celery slowly until just tender. Add turkey and heat thoroughly. Add tomato sauce and seasonings; simmer. Arrange bun halves on baking sheet. Spoon approximately ½ cup mixture over each. Top with a slice of cheese. Heat 5 minutes.

Salmon Spread

Makes approximately 1¼ cups.
Preparation Time: 10 minutes to mix; chill overnight.

- 1 7¾-ounce can salmon, drained and flaked
- 1 3-ounce package cream cheese, softened
- 2 tablespoons milk
- ¼ cup sweet pickle relish
- 3 tablespoons chopped green onions
- 2 tablespoons lemon juice

Combine ingredients; mix well. Chill overnight.

Sandwiches & Breads

California Rarebit

Makes 4 servings.
Preparation Time: 25 minutes.

    3 tablespoons butter
    ½ cup dry white wine
    2½ cups shredded Monterey Jack cheese
    1 egg, lightly beaten
    1 teaspoon Worcestershire sauce
    ½ teaspoon crushed basil
    2 cups sliced fresh mushrooms
    ½ teaspoon garlic salt
    4 slices pumpernickel bread, toasted

Melt 1 tablespoon butter in top of a double boiler. Add wine and heat; stir in 2 cups of cheese. Heat until melted. Add a little cheese mixture to egg; add back into cheese. Cook and stir about 1 minute. Add Worcestershire sauce and basil; keep warm. Sauté mushrooms in remaining butter just until tender. Sprinkle with garlic salt; remove from heat. Arrange toast on individual heatproof plates. Spoon sauce over toast; top with sautéed mushrooms. Sprinkle with remaining cheese. Broil until bubbly.

Cheesy Date Nut Loaf

Makes 1 loaf.
Preparation Time: 1 hour 40 minutes.

    ½ pound dates, finely chopped
    2 tablespoons butter
    ¾ cup boiling water
    1¾ cups sifted flour
    ¼ teaspoon salt
    1 teaspoon baking soda
    ½ cup granulated sugar
    1 egg, well-beaten
    4 ounces Cheddar cheese, shredded
    1 cup chopped walnuts

Preheat oven to 325°. Place dates and butter in small bowl. Pour boiling water over dates and butter. Let stand for 5 minutes. Sift dry ingredients together in large bowl. Add date mixture, egg, cheese and nuts. Mix until just blended. Spoon mixture into well-greased 9 x 5-inch loaf pan. Let stand for 20 minutes. Bake 50 to 60 minutes or until wooden pick inserted in center of loaf comes out clean. Turn out onto rack; cool.

Note: Flavor is improved if bread stands overnight before serving.

Cheese Bread Ring

Makes 1.
Preparation Time: 2 hours 45 minutes.

    2¾ to 3 cups flour
    2 tablespoons granulated sugar
    1 package active dry yeast
    ¾ teaspoon salt
    1 cup milk
    2 tablespoons butter
    1½ cups shredded sharp Cheddar cheese
        Butter

Combine 1½ cups flour, sugar, undissolved yeast and salt thoroughly in a large bowl. Heat together milk and butter until very warm. Gradually add to dry ingredients; beat 2 minutes at medium speed of mixer, scraping bowl occasionally. Add ½ cup flour and cheese. Beat 2 minutes at high speed, scraping bowl occasionally. Stir in enough additional flour to make a stiff dough. Turn out onto a lightly floured surface; knead until smooth and elastic, 5 to 8 minutes. Place in a greased bowl, turning to grease top. Cover; let rise in warm place until doubled in bulk, about 1 hour. Punch dough down. Turn out on lightly floured surface and shape to form one 20-inch rope. Place seam-side down in a buttered 6½-cup ring mold, pinching ends together. Cover; let rise in warm place until nearly doubled in bulk, 35 to 45 minutes. Bake in preheated 350° oven 25 to 30 minutes. Remove from ring mold.

Easter Egg Bread

Makes 2 large rings.
Preparation Time: 4 hours 30 minutes

    12 eggs
        Egg coloring
    ½ cup milk, scalded
    ½ cup granulated sugar
    1 teaspoon salt
    ½ cup butter
        Grated rinds of 2 lemons
    2 packages dry yeast
    ½ cup warm water
    2 eggs, lightly beaten
    4½ cups flour
    1 egg, beaten
        Tiny decorating candies

Wash the 12 eggs; tint shells with egg coloring and set aside. Add sugar, salt, butter and lemon rind to scalded milk. Cool to lukewarm. Dissolve yeast in warm water; add to milk mixture with 2 lightly beaten eggs and 2½ cups flour. Beat until smooth. Stir in enough remaining flour, a little at a time, to form a dough that is easy to handle. Turn onto a lightly floured board and knead until smooth and elastic, 5 to 8 minutes. Place in lightly greased bowl, turning to grease top. Cover and let rise in warm place until doubled in bulk, about 1½ hours. Punch down; let rise again, about ¾ hour. Divide into 4 parts. Form each part into a 36-inch rope. Shape 2 of the ropes into a very loosely braided ring, leaving space for 6 eggs. Place on greased baking sheet; pinch ends together. Repeat with other 2 ropes of dough for second ring. Insert colored eggs in each ring. Cover and let rise until doubled in bulk, about 1 hour. Brush with beaten egg. Sprinkle with decorating candies. Bake in a preheated 375° oven 20 minutes or until lightly browned. Serve warm.

Cheese Bread

Makes 2 1-pound loaves.
Preparation Time: 2 hours 20 minutes.

    5½ to 6 cups flour
    2 packages active dry yeast
    1 cup milk
    ¼ cup light corn syrup
    2 teaspoons salt
    2 tablespoons vegetable oil
    1 cup water
    4 ounces Cheddar cheese, shredded
      Vegetable oil

Preheat oven to 400°. Stir together 2 cups of flour and yeast in large bowl; set aside. Heat milk, corn syrup, salt, oil and water in saucepan over low heat until warm. Add liquid ingredients to flour-yeast mixture. Beat until smooth, about 3 minutes on medium speed of an electric mixer or 300 strokes by hand. Stir in shredded cheese. Gradually stir in enough flour to make a moderately soft dough. Turn out onto lightly floured surface. Knead until smooth and satiny, about 5 to 10 minutes. Cover dough with a bowl or towel and let stand for 20 minutes. Punch dough down; divide in half. Roll each half into a 14 x 7-inch rectangle. Roll up from narrow end, pressing dough into roll at each turn. Pinch ends together to seal; folds ends under loaf. Place in two greased 8 x 4-inch loaf pans. Brush tops with oil. Let rise in a warm place until doubled in bulk, about 30 to 45 minutes. Bake 35 to 40 minutes. Remove immediately from pans and brush tops with oil. Cool on wire rack.

Spoon Bread

Makes 4 to 6 servings.
Preparation Time: 1 hour 20 minutes.

    2 cups milk, scalded
    ½ cup cornmeal
    2 tablespoons butter *or* margarine
    3 eggs, separated
    1 teaspoon salt
    ½ teaspoon baking powder

Preheat oven to 375°. Set a 1½-quart casserole, greased only on the bottom, in a shallow baking pan; place in oven. Pour boiling water around casserole to depth of at least 1 inch; let casserole heat while Spoon Bread is prepared. Add cornmeal to scalded milk slowly, stirring constantly. Cook in top of double boiler over simmering water or in saucepan over low heat, 5 to 8 minutes. Blend in butter. Remove from heat and set aside. Beat egg yolks until thickened and lemon-colored. Stir cornmeal mixture into yolks. Add salt to egg whites and beat until stiff but not dry. Add baking powder; blend thoroughly. Fold cornmeal mixture into egg whites. Pour into heated casserole. Bake for 45 minutes or until a knife inserted halfway between center and outer edge comes out clean. Serve immediately by spoonfuls.

Giant Popovers

Makes 8.
Preparation Time: 1 hour 20 minutes.

    6 eggs
    2 cups milk
    6 tablespoons butter, melted
    2 cups flour
    1 teaspoon salt
    6 slices bacon, cooked, drained and crumbled

Preheat oven to 375°. Generously butter eight 6-ounce custard cups. Place cups in jelly-roll pan. Beat eggs lightly with electric mixer or rotary beater. Beat in milk and melted butter. Gradually beat in flour and salt. Stir in bacon. Divide batter among prepared custard cups. Bake 50 minutes. Remove from oven. Cut a slit in the side of each popover to let steam escape. Return to oven for 10 to 15 minutes, until tops are firm, crisp and deep brown.

To serve: Break hot popovers in half; spread with butter. For added flavor add minced green onion to butter.

Sandwiches & Breads

Apple Cheese Muffins

Makes 12 to 15.
Preparation Time: 1 hour.

- ½ cup shortening
- ½ cup granulated sugar
- 2 eggs
- 1½ cups flour
- 1 teaspoon baking powder
- 1 teaspoon baking soda
- ½ teaspoon salt
- ¾ cup quick-cooking rolled oats
- 1 cup finely chopped apples
- ⅔ cup coarsely grated sharp Cheddar cheese
- ½ cup chopped pecans
- ¾ cup milk
- 12 to 15 thin slices unpeeled red apple
  Melted butter or margarine
  Cinnamon-sugar

Preheat oven to 400°. Cream shortening and sugar together. Add eggs, one at a time, beating well after each addition. Combine flour, baking powder, baking soda and salt in mixing bowl; mix lightly. Gradually stir flour mixture into shortening mixture. In this order add oats, apples, cheese and pecans, mixing well after each addition. Gradually add milk, stirring until all ingredients are just moistened. Grease muffin pans. Fill each cup two-thirds full of batter. Dip apple slices in melted butter, then in cinnamon-sugar. Press 1 apple slice into top of each muffin. Sprinkle lightly with cinnamon-sugar. Bake 25 minutes or until golden brown.

Pot-Cheese Dumplings

Makes 4 servings.
Preparation Time: 25 minutes.

- 1 pound dry pot cheese
- 2 eggs
- 1 cup flour
- 1 teaspoon salt
- 3 quarts boiling water
- ½ cup butter or margarine, melted
- ½ pint sour cream
  Parsley or paprika, optional

Mash cheese; add eggs; mix well. Stir in flour and salt. Drop by tablespoonfuls into rapidly boiling water; cover and boil 15 minutes. Drain; serve with melted butter and sour cream. Sprinkle with parsley or paprika, if desired.

Cottage Cheese Butter Horns

Makes 36.
Preparation Time: 10 minutes to mix; chill overnight; 40 minutes to prepare and bake.

- 2 cups flour
- ½ teaspoon salt
- 12 ounces creamed cottage cheese
- 1 cup butter, softened

Cream all ingredients together; cover; refrigerate overnight. Divide dough into three equal sections. Keep at room temperature until easy to handle. On a floured board roll each section into a 10-inch round. Cut each circle into 12 pie-shaped pieces. Roll up from wide end to tip. Bake on lightly buttered cookie sheets 30 minutes at 350°. Cool. Serve plain or frost with Glaze.

Glaze

- ⅓ cup butter
- 2 cups confectioners' sugar
- 1½ teaspoons vanilla or lemon extract
- 2 to 4 tablespoons hot water

Melt butter in saucepan. Blend in sugar and flavoring. Stir in water, 1 tablespoon at a time, until smooth.

Cheesabutter

Makes 1¼ cups.
Preparation Time: 10 minutes.

- ½ cup butter, softened
- ¾ teaspoon Italian seasoning
- ⅛ teaspoon garlic powder
- ⅛ teaspoon pepper
- 1 cup shredded Cheddar cheese
- 1 teaspoon fresh lemon juice

Beat butter and seasonings until fluffy. Blend in cheese and lemon juice. Form into a log. Wrap in waxed paper; refrigerate until ready to use. Good on corn on the cob, baked potatoes, hamburgers, steak or hot bread.

Scandinavian Egg Butter

Makes approximately 1 cup.
Preparation Time: 10 minutes.

- ½ cup butter, softened
- ½ teaspoon salt
- ⅛ teaspoon pepper
- 3 hard-cooked eggs, peeled
  Warm toast

Whip butter until fluffy. Beat in salt and pepper. Mash eggs with a fork. Gently fold into butter. Serve on warm toast.

Desserts

Sensational Sponge Custard

Makes 6 servings.
Preparation Time: 1 hour 15 minutes.

    1 11-ounce can mixed pineapple tidbits and
      mandarin orange segments, drained, reserve syrup
    ⅓ cup granulated sugar
    3 tablespoons flour
    3 eggs, separated
    ½ cup milk
    2 tablespoons rum
    1½ tablespoons butter, melted
    ¼ teaspoon cream of tartar

Preheat oven to 350°. Place 2 to 3 tablespoons fruit in each of 6 6-ounce custard cups. Combine sugar and flour in bowl. Stir in reserved syrup, egg yolks, milk, rum and butter; blend well. Beat egg whites and cream of tartar in large bowl until stiff but not dry. Fold yolk mixture gently into egg whites. Pour into custard cups. Set cups in a 13 x 9 x 2-inch baking pan. Pour very hot water into pan to within ½ inch of top of custard cups. Bake 30 to 35 minutes or until cake tester inserted into center comes out clean. Remove promptly from hot water. Cool at least 5 minutes before serving or cool completely.

To Microwave: Prepare custard mixture as above. Set custard cups in 11 x 7 x 1½-inch baking dish. Pour very hot water into dish to within ½ inch of top of custard cups. Microwave 20 minutes on Defrost, rotating dish ½ turn every 2 minutes, or until cake tester inserted into center comes out clean. Remove promptly from hot water.

Lemony Cake Top Pudding

Makes 6 servings.
Preparation Time: 1 hour 30 minutes.

    4 eggs, separated
    1 cup granulated sugar
    3 tablespoons butter *or* margarine, softened
    3 tablespoons flour
    ¼ teaspoon salt
    ⅓ cup fresh lemon juice
    1 cup milk
    2 teaspoons grated fresh lemon peel
    ¼ cup sliced almonds

Preheat oven to 325°. Beat egg whites in small bowl with electric mixer until foamy; gradually add ¼ cup sugar, beating until soft peaks form. Set aside. Beat egg yolks and butter in large bowl, using same beaters. Gradually add remaining ¾ cup sugar, beating until well blended, about 5 minutes. Add flour, salt and lemon juice; mix well. Blend in milk and lemon peel. Gently fold in egg whites. Sprinkle almonds over bottom of buttered 1½-quart casserole; pour in batter. Set casserole in shallow pan filled with ½-inch hot water. Bake 55 to 60 minutes or until lightly browned. Serve warm or chilled.

Old-Fashioned Baked Rice Pudding

Makes 6 to 8 servings.
Preparation Time: 1 hour 10 minutes; chill if desired.

    4 eggs, beaten
    3 cups milk
    ⅓ cup granulated sugar
    ¼ teaspoon salt
    2 teaspoons vanilla extract
    2 teaspoons grated lemon peel
    2 cups cooked rice
    ½ cup seedless raisins

Preheat oven to 300°. Combine all ingredients and pour into a 2½-quart baking dish. Set dish in pan of hot water. Bake 30 minutes; insert spoon at edge of pudding and stir from bottom. Continue baking 30 minutes or until knife inserted into center of pudding comes out clean. Serve hot or cold.

Eggnog Tapioca

Makes 6 servings.
Preparation Time: 35 minutes.

    2 eggs, separated
    4 tablespoons granulated sugar
    2 cups milk
    3 tablespoons quick-cooking tapioca
    ⅛ teaspoon salt
    1 teaspoon rum flavoring
      Nutmeg

Beat egg yolks; add 2 tablespoons sugar and ½ cup milk; blend well. Add tapioca and remaining milk. Cook over low heat, stirring constantly, until mixture boils. Remove from heat; cool. Add salt and flavoring. Beat egg whites until foamy; gradually add remaining 2 tablespoons sugar, beating constantly until stiff peaks form. Fold into tapioca mixture. Pour into serving dish; chill. Sprinkle with nutmeg.

Fresh Strawberries with Creamy Dip

Makes 8 servings.
Preparation Time: 1 hour 10 minutes.

    1 8-ounce package cream cheese, softened
    1 cup dairy sour cream
    ⅓ cup confectioners' sugar
    2 teaspoons orange liqueur
    1 quart fresh strawberries, washed and hulled

Beat cream cheese, sour cream, confectioners' sugar and orange liqueur in bowl until smooth. Chill 1 hour. Fill 8 cordial glasses or tiny cups with Creamy Dip. Place each on dessert plate and serve with whole berries.

Whipped Cheese Topping

Makes 1⅓ cups.
Preparation Time: 5 minutes.

    2 cups shredded Cheddar cheese, room temperature
    ¼ cup milk

Beat cheese in a bowl until fairly smooth; gradually add milk and continue to beat until mixture is smooth and fluffy.

Serving suggestions: Serve over hot fruit pie, warm gingerbread or spice cake or as a spread on sliced apples or pears.

Cream Puffs with Creamy-Cot Filling

Makes 1 dozen.
Preparation Time: 1 hour.

    1 cup water
    ½ cup butter or margarine
    1 cup flour
    4 eggs
      Maraschino cherries, optional
      Mint leaves, optional

Preheat oven to 400°. Heat water and butter to boiling in large saucepan. Add flour, stirring vigorously over low heat for about ½ minute or until mixture forms a ball. Remove from heat. Add eggs, all at the same time; beat until smooth. Use a scant ¼ cup dough for each cream puff. Drop dough 3 inches apart onto ungreased baking sheet. Bake 25 minutes or until puffed and golden. Remove at once from baking sheet. Cool. Cut off top third of each cream puff shortly before serving time; remove excess soft dough. Place 1½ tablespoons chilled Apricot Filling in each cream puff; replace tops. Drizzle Glaze over top of each cream puff. Garnish with a sliver of red maraschino cherry and a sprig of fresh mint, if desired.

Apricot Filling

    1 16-ounce can apricot halves, drained
    ⅔ cup granulated sugar
    ¼ teaspoon ground cinnamon
    1 cup dairy sour cream

Purée apricots in blender or food processor. Stir puréed apricots and sugar together in medium saucepan. Bring mixture to a boil; simmer, uncovered, about 15 minutes until thickened. Cool mixture; stir in cinnamon and sour cream. Chill.

Glaze

    1 cup confectioners' sugar
    2 to 3 tablespoons milk or cream

Blend confectioners' sugar and enough milk to make a smooth glaze.

Cool Creamy Cheese Squares

Makes 9 servings.
Preparation Time: 20 minutes; chill 2 hours or overnight.

    2 tablespoons margarine or butter
    2 tablespoons granulated sugar
    ¼ teaspoon cinnamon
    ½ cup cornflake crumbs
    1 8-ounce package cream cheese, softened
    ½ cup granulated sugar
    ⅛ teaspoon salt
    1 tablespoon reconstituted lemon juice
    1 teaspoon vanilla extract
    1½ cups whipped cream or frozen nondairy
      topping, thawed

Melt margarine over low heat in saucepan. Add 2 tablespoons sugar and cinnamon. Cook, stirring constantly, over low heat until mixture becomes syrupy and begins to bubble. Remove from heat. Add cornflake crumbs; mix well. Set aside. Beat cream cheese until smooth and fluffy in small bowl. Add ½ cup sugar and salt gradually, beating constantly. Mix in lemon juice and vanilla. Fold in whipped cream just until combined. Spoon cream cheese mixture into ungreased 8 x 8 x 2-inch pan. Sprinkle crumb mixture evenly over top, pressing in lightly with back of spoon. Freeze until firm. Cut into squares.

Desserts

Cherry Cheesecake Parfaits

Makes 6 servings.
Preparation Time: 20 minutes.

- 12 ounces cream cheese, softened
- 2 cups cold milk
- ¼ cup granulated sugar
- ½ teaspoon vanilla
- 1 3¾-ounce package instant vanilla pudding and pie filling
- 1 16-ounce can pitted sour red cherries, thoroughly drained
- ½ cup graham cracker crumbs
- 1 tablespoon granulated sugar
- 1 tablespoon butter, melted

Beat cream cheese until light and fluffy. Blend in ½ cup of milk. Add remaining milk, ¼ cup sugar, vanilla and pudding and pie filling. Beat slowly with rotary beater or at lowest speed of an electric mixer until thoroughly blended, about 2 minutes. Fold cherries into pudding mixture. Combine graham cracker crumbs, remaining sugar and melted butter in separate bowl. Alternately layer pudding and crumb mixtures in parfait glasses. Chill thoroughly before serving.

Mocha Cheesecake

Makes 10 to 12 servings.
Preparation Time: 1 hour 45 minutes.

Crust

- 1½ cups chocolate cookie crumbs
- ¼ cup ground nuts
- ⅓ cup butter, melted

Preheat oven to 325°. Combine all ingredients. Press onto bottom and halfway up sides of a 9-inch springform pan. Bake 8 to 10 minutes. Cool on wire rack while preparing Filling.

Filling

- 1 tablespoon instant coffee dissolved in 3 tablespoons hot water
- 6 ounces sweet chocolate
- 3 eggs
- ¾ cup granulated sugar
- 3 3-ounce packages cream cheese
- 1 cup whipping cream
- ⅓ cup sifted flour
- ¼ teaspoon salt
- ⅛ teaspoon baking soda
- 1 teaspoon vanilla
  Whipped cream
  Chocolate curls

Pour coffee into saucepan; add chocolate and melt over low heat, stirring frequently; set aside.

Beat eggs until fluffy and light in color. Gradually add sugar to eggs, beating well after each addition; set aside. Beat cream cheese until fluffy; add whipping cream and continue to beat until mixture is thickened and will mound when dropped from a spoon. Fold in chocolate mixture. Fold in egg mixture. Sift dry ingredients; stir into batter; blend in vanilla. Pour into baked Crust. Bake until filling is set, about 65 to 70 minutes. Cool completely on wire rack. Refrigerate overnight. Place on serving plate; remove sides of pan. Garnish with whipped cream and chocolate curls.

Cranberry Cheesecake

Makes 10 to 12 servings.

Preparation Time: 1 hour 30 minutes.

- 1½ cups graham cracker crumbs
- 1¼ cups granulated sugar
- ½ teaspoon cinnamon
- ⅓ cup butter, melted
- 3 8-ounce packages cream cheese, softened
- 5 eggs
- ¼ teaspoon salt
- 1 teaspoon vanilla

Preheat oven to 350°. Mix graham cracker crumbs, ¼ cup sugar and cinnamon; stir in butter. Press mixture firmly and evenly onto the bottom of a 9-inch springform pan or 13 x 9-inch pan. Beat cream cheese until soft and fluffy. Gradually beat in 1 cup sugar. Add eggs; blend until smooth. Beat in salt and vanilla. Pour mixture into crust. Bake 45 minutes or until firm and slightly puffed. Cool cake in oven (*Note:* A crack in cake is characteristic.) Remove from oven and chill.

Topping

- 1 tablespoon cornstarch
- ½ cup granulated sugar
- ½ cup water
- 1½ cups fresh cranberries, rinsed and drained

Mix cornstarch, ½ cup sugar and water in saucepan until smooth; add cranberries. Cook over low heat, stirring constantly, until mixture bubbles and thickens. Simmer, stirring constantly for 2 minutes. Cool. Spread Topping on top of cheesecake. Chill until ready to serve.

Desserts

Superb Cheesecake

Makes 10 to 12 servings.
Preparation Time: 3 hours 20 minutes; 3 to 4 hours to chill.

    3 tablespoons cornstarch
    3 tablespoons flour
      Grated peel of 1 lemon
      Juice of 1 lemon
    1 teaspoon vanilla
   16 ounces cream-style small curd cottage cheese
    2 8-ounce packages cream cheese, softened
 1½ cups granulated sugar
    4 eggs
   ½ cup butter, melted
    2 8-ounce cartons plain yogurt
      Cherry or blueberry pie filling, optional

Preheat oven to 325°. Combine cornstarch, flour, lemon peel, lemon juice and vanilla; set aside. Combine cottage cheese and cream cheese in mixing bowl; beat until thoroughly blended. Beat in sugar. Beat in eggs, one at a time. Blend in melted butter and yogurt. Blend in cornstarch mixture. Spoon mixture into a buttered 9-inch springform. Bake for 60 to 70 minutes or until firm around edges. Turn off heat. Let cake stand in oven for 2 hours. Remove from oven. Refrigerate until thoroughly chilled, 3 to 4 hours. Serve plain or topped with pie filling.

Festive Chocolate Cheesecake

Makes 10 to 12 servings.
Preparation Time: 1 hour 40 minutes.

    1 cup graham cracker crumbs
    3 tablespoons granulated sugar
    3 tablespoons butter, melted
    2 cups semisweet chocolate morsels
    2 8-ounce packages cream cheese, softened
    2 eggs
   ¾ cup granulated sugar
    2 tablespoons flour
    1 teaspoon vanilla
   ½ cup heavy cream, whipped
   ½ cup mandarin orange sections, drained
   ¼ cup maraschino cherries, drained and cut in half

Preheat oven to 350°. In small bowl, combine graham cracker crumbs, sugar and butter; blend thoroughly. Press mixture into the bottom of a 9-inch springform. Place chocolate in small saucepan. Melt over hot, *not boiling,* water. Remove from heat; set aside. In large bowl beat cream cheese until smooth. Add eggs, sugar, flour and vanilla; beat until thoroughly blended. Blend in melted chocolate. Pour into graham cracker crust. Bake for 1 hour and 15 minutes. Cool completely in pan before removing rim. Spread whipped cream over top. Decorate with mandarin orange sections and maraschino cherry halves. Refrigerate until ready to serve.

Sponge Cake

Makes 10 to 12 servings.
Preparation Time: 1 hour.

    6 eggs
   ¾ teaspoon cream of tartar
 1½ cups granulated sugar
 1½ cups flour
    1 tablespoon grated orange or lemon peel
    1 teaspoon baking powder
   ½ teaspoon salt
   ½ cup water
    1 teaspoon vanilla
      Fruit and whipped cream or Seven Minute Frosting

Preheat oven to 350°. Separate eggs, placing whites in large bowl and yolks in small bowl. Add cream of tartar to egg whites; beat until mixture forms soft peaks. Gradually add ¾ cup sugar, 2 tablespoons at a time, beating at high speed until stiff peaks form. Add flour, remaining ¾ cup sugar, orange peel, baking powder, salt, water and vanilla to egg yolks. Blend at low speed until moistened; beat 1 minute at medium speed. Pour yolk mixture over egg whites; fold in gently just until blended. Pour batter into ungreased 10-inch tube pan. Bake 40 to 45 minutes or until top springs back when lightly touched. Invert tube pan on funnel or soft drink bottle; cool completely. Serve with fruit and whipped cream or frost with Seven Minute Frosting.

Seven Minute Frosting

Makes 5 cups.
Preparation Time: 10 minutes.

    2 egg whites
 1½ cups granulated sugar
   ⅓ cup cold water
   ⅛ teaspoon cream of tartar
   ⅛ teaspoon salt
    1 teaspoon vanilla

Combine all ingredients except vanilla in large saucepan. Beat 1 minute at low speed with hand mixer. Place pan over low heat; beat at high speed until stiff peaks form, about 5 minutes. Remove from heat. Add vanilla. Beat until frosting will hold swirls, about 2 minutes longer.

Cocoa Chiffon Cake

Makes 10 to 12 servings.
Preparation Time: 1 hour 30 minutes; 1 hour to cool.

    ¾ cup boiling water
    ½ cup cocoa
    1¾ cups flour
    1½ cups granulated sugar
    3 teaspoons baking powder
    1 teaspoon salt
    ½ cup vegetable oil
    7 egg yolks
    1 teaspoon vanilla
    ¼ teaspoon red food coloring
    1 cup egg whites (7 or 8)
    ½ teaspoon cream of tartar

Preheat oven to 325°. Combine water and cocoa; stir until smooth. Set aside to cool. Combine flour, sugar, baking powder and salt in mixing bowl. Make a well in center. Add cooled cocoa mixture, oil, egg yolks, vanilla and food coloring. Mix with spoon until smooth. In large mixing bowl, beat egg whites and cream of tartar until very stiff peaks form. *Do not underbeat.* Pour flour mixture slowly over egg whites; fold just until blended. *Do not stir.* Carefully pour mixture into an ungreased 10-inch tube pan. Bake for 55 minutes; then increase temperature to 350°. Bake 10 to 15 minutes or until the top springs back when lightly touched. Turn pan upside-down over neck of a funnel or bottle. Let stand until cool. Loosen cake from sides of pan with a spatula. Frost with your favorite fluffy white frosting.

Note: Best made when it is not humid.

Apple-Cream Cheese Bars

Makes 24 bars.
Preparation Time: 1 hour 45 minutes.

Crust

    2 cups flour
    3 tablespoons granulated sugar
    1 teaspoon salt
    ⅓ cup cold butter
    3 tablespoons vegetable oil
    1 small egg
    2⅔ tablespoons cold water

Combine flour, sugar and salt in mixing bowl. Cut in butter with pastry blender or two knives until mixture resembles coarse crumbs. Blend in oil, egg and cold water until mixture is just blended. Gather dough into a ball. Roll out on lightly floured surface into a 12 x 18-inch rectangle. Ease dough into an ungreased jelly-roll pan.

Filling

    6 cups pared and sliced baking apples
    1 cup granulated sugar
    ½ cup flour
    2 teaspoons grated lemon rind
    1 tablespoon lemon juice
    1 cup evaporated milk
   40 caramels
    1 8-ounce package cream cheese, softened
    1 egg
    ⅓ cup granulated sugar
    ½ cup chopped nuts

Preheat oven to 325°. Combine the apples, sugar, flour, lemon rind and lemon juice; mix lightly. Spoon apple mixture into crust. Combine milk and caramels in a saucepan. Cook over low heat until caramels are melted, stirring often. Pour the caramel mixture over apples. Combine the cream cheese, egg and sugar; blend thoroughly. Spoon cream cheese mixture over caramel topping. Sprinkle nuts over top. Bake 55 minutes. Cool in pan. Cut into 3-inch bars.

Cottage Cheese-Fudge Cupcakes

Makes 24.
Preparation Time: 1 hour.

    ½ cup coffee, boiling
    ½ cup cocoa
    1¾ cups granulated sugar
    ⅔ cup butter, softened
    2 eggs
    1 teaspoon vanilla
    2½ cups flour
    1½ teaspoons baking soda
    ½ teaspoon salt
    ½ cup buttermilk
    ½ cup creamed cottage cheese, sieved

Preheat oven to 350°. Add coffee to cocoa; stir until smooth and set aside. Cream sugar and butter until light and fluffy. Add eggs, 1 at a time, beating well after each addition. Beat in vanilla and cocoa mixture. Mix flour, baking soda and salt together. Blend buttermilk and sieved cottage cheese; add alternately with sifted dry ingredients to batter; beat well. Spoon batter into buttered muffin pans. Bake 15 to 20 minutes or until a toothpick inserted in center comes out clean.

Zucchini Cake

Makes 10 to 12 servings.
Preparation Time: 50 minutes.

  1 cup vegetable oil
  2 cups granulated sugar
  4 eggs
  2 cups peeled, grated zucchini
  2 cups flour
  1 teaspoon baking soda
  ½ teaspoon salt
  1 teaspoon cinnamon
  ½ cup chopped marachino cherries
  ½ cup chopped nuts, optional

Preheat oven to 350°. Mix oil and sugar; beat in eggs. Stir in zucchini. Add dry ingredients; mix well. Stir in cherries and nuts. Pour into a greased and floured 13 x 9-inch baking pan. Bake for 30 minutes.

Basic Meringue

Makes topping for 1 9-inch pastry.
Preparation Time: 30 minutes; cool 2 hours.

  4 egg whites, at room temperature
  ¼ teaspoon cream of tartar
  8 tablespoons granulated sugar

Beat whites with electric mixer in small deep bowl several seconds until frothy. Add cream of tartar. Beat at high speed until whites begin to lose foamy appearance and form soft peaks. Reduce speed to medium. Add sugar gradually, 1 tablespoon at a time. Return to high speed and beat until whites are fairly stiff and glossy. Place meringue on hot pie; cover pie by swirling meringue from edge to edge, sealing completely and forming decorative peaks. Bake at 350° for 12 to 15 minutes until golden brown. Cool on wire rack at room temperature (away from drafts) for 2 hours. Use sharp knife to cut; dip into hot water after each cut for clean edges.

Individual Meringues

Makes 10 to 12.
Preparation Time: 2 hours 20 minutes

  1 teaspoon cream of tartar
  ½ teaspoon salt
  4 egg whites
  1 cup granulated sugar
  Fresh fruit

Preheat oven to 225°. Add cream of tartar and salt to egg whites; beat until stiff peaks form. Add sugar, 1 tablespoon at a time, beating well after each addition. Shape meringue with a spoon or pastry bag on baking sheet lined with several thicknesses of ungreased brown paper. Make each about 3 inches in diameter, building up edge to form a rim. Bake 70 minutes. Cool meringues thoroughly before removing from paper. Serve with fresh strawberries or other fresh fruit in season.

Apple Meringue Pie

Makes 8 to 10 servings.
Preparation Time: 1 hour 15 minutes.

  1 unbaked 9-inch pastry shell or 1 22-ounce
    package piecrust mix
  1 cup granulated sugar
  2 tablespoons cornstarch
  ½ teaspoon cinnamon
  ½ teaspoon nutmeg
  3 egg yolks
  3 tablespoons butter, melted
  ½ cup light cream
  2½ cups shredded unpared tart apples
  ½ cup raisins
    Meringue

Preheat oven to 400°. Prepare pastry for 9-inch pie; line pie pan. Stir sugar, cornstarch and spices together. Beat egg yolks until thick and lem-on-colored in small bowl. Gradually beat in sugar-spice mixture, butter and cream. Fold in apples and raisins. Pour into pie pan. Cover edge with 2- to 3-inch strip of aluminum foil to prevent excessive browning; remove foil last 15 minutes of baking. Bake 35 to 40 minutes or until set. Cover pie with meringue while hot, carefully sealing meringue onto edge of crust. Bake 8 to 10 minutes longer. Cool on wire rack away from draft.

Meringue

  3 egg whites
  ¼ teaspoon cream of tartar
  6 tablespoons granulated sugar
  ½ teaspoon vanilla

Beat egg whites and cream of tartar until frothy. Beat in sugar, 1 tablespoon at a time; continue beating until stiff and glossy. *Do not underbeat.* Beat in vanilla.

Desserts

Orange Swirls

Makes 6 servings.
Preparation Time: 1 hour 30 minutes; chill overnight.

Meringue

  3 egg whites
¼ teaspoon cream of tartar
⅛ teaspoon salt
¾ cup granulated sugar

Preheat oven to 275°. Beat egg whites until foamy; add cream of tartar and salt; beat until stiff but not dry. Gradually add sugar, beating until very stiff. Cover baking sheet with heavy brown paper or aluminum foil. Shape meringue, with spoon or pastry bag, into 6 rounds about 3 inches in diameter on baking sheet. Make a 2-inch diameter depression in center of each. Bake 1 hour. Cool.

Orange Filling

  3 egg yolks
  2 tablespoons granulated sugar
⅛ teaspoon salt
  6 tablespoons frozen orange concentrate,
      thawed and undiluted
1½ teaspoons grated orange rind
  1 cup heavy cream, whipped
  6 orange sections

Beat egg yolks in top of double boiler. Add sugar, salt and orange juice concentrate. Cook over boiling water, stirring constantly, until thickened. Remove from heat; add orange rind and chill. Fold in whipped cream. Spoon into meringues. Chill 12 to 24 hours. Garnish with orange sections.

Old-Fashioned Lemon Meringue Pie

Makes 8 to 10 servings.
Preparation Time: 1 hour.

  1 baked 9-inch pastry shell
  1 cup plus 2 tablespoons granulated sugar
¼ cup plus 3 tablespoons flour
⅛ teaspoon salt
  1 cup water
  4 egg yolks, well beaten
  1 teaspoon grated fresh lemon peel
½ cup fresh lemon juice
  2 tablespoons butter
1½ cups milk, scalded
      Few drops yellow food coloring
      Meringue (Recipe on page 59)

Preheat oven to 350°. Combine sugar, flour and salt in heavy saucepan; blend in water until

smooth. Blend in yolks, lemon peel, lemon juice and butter. Stir in hot milk gradually. Bring to a boil over medium heat, stirring constantly with a rubber spatula to avoid scorching. Boil 5 minutes, stirring constantly. Blend in food coloring; cool. Prepare Meringue. Pour filling into baked pastry shell. Top with Meringue, sealing well at edges. Bake 12 to 15 minutes. Cool on wire rack away from drafts.

Peanut Meringue Kisses

Makes 2 dozen.
Preparation Time: 2 hours 45 minutes.

  2 egg whites
⅛ teaspoon cream of tartar
½ cup granulated sugar
½ cup finely chopped peanuts
  3 tablespoons milk
  1 ounce unsweetened chocolate
  1 teaspoon butter
⅓ cup confectioners' sugar
¼ cup peanut butter
½ teaspoon vanilla

Preheat oven to 200°. In small mixing bowl beat egg whites and cream of tartar until frothy. Gradually add granulated sugar, beating until stiff peaks form. Cover large baking sheet with aluminum foil. Using a teaspoon, drop 48 spoonfuls of meringue mixture onto prepared baking sheet. Lightly press chopped peanuts onto outside of each meringue. Bake for 1 hour and 20 minutes or until meringues are crisp and dry. Remove from oven and cool thoroughly. Place milk, chocolate and butter in a saucepan. Cook, stirring over low heat until chocolate is melted. Beat in confectioners' sugar, peanut butter and vanilla. Spread chocolate filling evenly on bottoms of 24 meringues. Press bottoms of remaining meringues onto filling.

Raisin Kisses

Makes 3 dozen.
Preparation Time: 1 hour.

  4 egg whites
¼ teaspoon salt
  1 cup granulated sugar
  1 teaspoon vanilla
  2 cups cornflakes
  1 cup raisins, coarsely chopped
½ cup flaked coconut

Preheat oven to 350°. Beat egg whites with salt until soft peaks form. Gradually add sugar, beating until very stiff but not dry. Beat in vanilla. Fold in cornflakes, raisins and coconut. Drop mixture, using a teaspoon, onto lightly greased cookie sheets. Bake 20 to 25 minutes or until set and golden brown. Immediately remove from cookie sheet to racks to cool.

Salted Peanut Cookies

Makes 6 dozen.
Preparation Time: 45 minutes.

    1 cup butter *or* margarine
    1 cup granulated sugar
    1 cup dark brown sugar
    2 eggs
    1 teaspoon vanilla
 1½ cups flour
    1 teaspoon baking soda
    3 cups uncooked oats
 1½ cups salted peanuts

Preheat oven to 375°. Cream butter and sugars. Add eggs and vanilla; beat until fluffy. Sift flour with soda; add oats. Stir dry ingredients into batter. Add peanuts; mix well. Drop, using a teaspoon, onto ungreased cookie sheets. Bake 12 minutes. Cool on wire rack.

Raisin Cheesecake Cookies

Makes approximately 3 dozen.
Preparation Time: 2 hours 30 minutes.

 ⅓ cup butter, softened
 ⅓ cup brown sugar, firmly packed
  1 cup flour
 ½ cup raisins
 ½ cup chopped walnuts
  1 8-ounce package cream cheese, softened
 ¼ cup granulated sugar
  1 egg
  2 tablespoons milk
  1 tablespoon lemon juice
 ½ teaspoon vanilla

Preheat oven to 350°. Cream butter and brown sugar together in bowl until fluffy. Add flour, raisins and walnuts. Blend mixture with fork until crumbly. Reserve 1 cup of mixture and lightly press remainder into greased 8-inch square pan. Bake 15 minutes or until golden at edges. Cool. Mix cream cheese and sugar together in bowl until well blended. Add egg, milk, lemon juice and vanilla; beat until smooth. Spread mixture over cooled crust; sprinkle reserved raisin-nut mixture over top. Bake 25 to 30 minutes or until center is firm. Cool at room temperature; cover and chill 1 hour or until serving time.

Cheesecake Pear Pie

Makes 6 to 8 servings.
Preparation Time: 1 hour 30 minutes.

    1 9-inch unbaked pastry shell
    6 tablespoons margarine *or* butter
 ½ cup granulated sugar
    1 cup dairy sour cream
 ¾ cup flour
    1 teaspoon vanilla extract
 ¼ teaspoon salt
    2 eggs
    1 16-ounce can Bartlett pear halves, drained
 ½ cup shredded Cheddar cheese
 ⅓ cup firmly packed brown sugar
 ¼ teaspoon nutmeg
      Confectioners' sugar, optional

Preheat oven to 400°. Prepare pastry shell; set aside. Cream 2 tablespoons margarine with sugar until light and fluffy. Add sour cream, ¼ cup flour, vanilla, salt and eggs; beat until well blended. Arrange pear halves, cut side up, in pastry shell. Sprinkle with cheese; pour custard mixture into shell. Bake 30 minutes. Combine remaining ½ cup flour, brown sugar and nutmeg; cut in remaining 4 tablespoons margarine. Remove pie from oven; sprinkle with crumbs. Bake an additional 10 minutes. Serve warm or cold. Sprinkle with confectioners' sugar, if desired.

Creamy Pumpkin-Ricotta Pie

Makes 8 to 10 servings.
Preparation Time: 1 hour 30 minutes.

    1 unbaked 9-inch pastry shell
    2 eggs
    1 cup ricotta cheese
    1 16-ounce can pumpkin
 ¾ cup light brown sugar, firmly packed
 ½ teaspoon salt
 1½ teaspoons pumpkin pie spice
    1 teaspoon vanilla
    1 5⅓-ounce can evaporated milk
      Vanilla yogurt, optional
      Pumpkin seeds, optional

Preheat oven to 375°. Beat eggs lightly in a large bowl; beat in cheese until smooth. Stir in remaining 6 ingredients until well blended. Pour into prepared pastry shell. Bake 45 minutes. Cool completely on wire rack. Garnish with yogurt and pumpkin seeds, if desired. Keep refrigerated.

Creme de Menthe Alaska Pie

Makes 10 to 12 servings.
Preparation Time: 1 hour 15 minutes.

Crust

1¼ cups chocolate wafer crumbs
¼ cup butter, melted

Preheat oven to 350°. Combine crumbs and butter; blend thoroughly. Press firmly into bottom and sides of a 9-inch pie plate that is freezer to oven safe. Bake 6 to 8 minutes. Cool to room temperature. Freeze until firm.

Filling

3 pints vanilla ice cream, slightly softened
¼ cup creme de menthe
6 tablespoons chocolate wafer crumbs

Spread 1 pint of ice cream over bottom of crust. Drizzle with 2 tablespoons of creme de menthe. Sprinkle on 2 tablespoons of wafer crumbs. Repeat for remaining ice cream, creme de menthe and crumbs. Press top layer of crumbs firmly into ice cream. Freeze until firm.

Meringue

4 egg whites at room temperature
¼ teaspoon cream of tartar
½ cup granulated sugar
½ teaspoon vanilla

Beat egg whites and cream of tartar until soft peaks form. Add sugar, 1 tablespoon at a time, beating constantly until whites are glossy and stiff peaks form. Beat in vanilla.

Assemble

Preheat oven to 475°. Spread Meringue over ice cream to edges of crust, being careful to cover all of ice cream.* Place pie on a bread or pizza board. Bake on rack at lowest oven position for 3 to 5 minutes or until lightly browned. Watch carefully to avoid overbrowning.

*Can be made ahead to this point and frozen for 24 hours.

Pineapple Chiffon Pie

Makes 6 to 8 servings.
Preparation Time: 2 hours 45 minutes.

1 envelope unflavored gelatin
¾ cup granulated sugar
⅛ teaspoon salt
4 eggs, separated
1¼ cups canned pineapple juice
¼ cup lemon juice
½ cup heavy cream, whipped
1 baked 9-inch pastry shell

Combine gelatin, ¼ cup sugar and salt in top of double boiler. Combine egg yolks and pineapple juice in small bowl. Beat until lemon colored. Stir into gelatin. Cook over boiling water, stirring constantly, until mixture thickens slightly and gelatin dissolves, 5 to 7 minutes. Remove from heat. Add lemon juice. Place mixture in mixing bowl. Set bowl in larger container filled with ice cubes. Cool, stirring occasionally until mixture mounds when dropped from a spoon. Beat egg whites until foamy. Gradually add remaining ½ cup sugar; beat until stiff peaks form. Fold gelatin mixture into egg white mixture. Fold in whipped cream. Spoon into pastry shell. Chill until set, at least 2 hours.

Blueberry-Cream Cheese Pie

Makes 8 to 10 servings.
Preparation Time: 1 hour 5 minutes.

1 unbaked 9-inch pastry shell
12 ounces cream cheese, softened
2 tablespoons flour
3 eggs, separated
3 tablespoons granulated sugar
½ teaspoon salt
¾ cup sour cream
1½ cups fresh blueberries, rinsed and drained

Preheat oven to 350°. Stir cream cheese with fork until smooth. Mix in 1 tablespoon flour. Lightly beat egg yolks. Reserve 2 teaspoons egg white. Beat remaining egg whites until soft peaks form. Add to beaten yolks. Add sugar, salt and sour cream. Combine egg mixture with cream cheese mixture, blending well. Brush unbaked pie shell lightly with reserved egg white. Dredge blueberries in remaining flour. Place berries in pie shell. Smooth cream cheese mixture evenly over berries. Bake 45 minutes or until topping is set.

Index

A B C D E F G H I J K L
2 3 4 5 6 7 8 9 0 1